FINANCE AND THE INTERNATIONAL ECONOMY
6

The Prize Winning Essays from the first five competitions have been published in the following Oxford University Press volumes:

Finance and the International Economy (The 1987 Essays)
eds. John Calverley and Richard O'Brien

International Economics and Financial Markets (The 1988 Essays)
eds. Richard O'Brien and Tapan Datta

Finance and the International Economy: 3 (The 1989 Essays)
eds. Richard O'Brien and Ingrid Iversen

Finance and the International Economy: 4 (The 1990 Essays)
eds. Richard O'Brien and Sarah Hewin

Finance and the International Economy: 5 (The 1991 Essays)
ed. Richard O'Brien

Finance and the
International Economy
6

The AMEX Bank Review
Prize Essays

In Memory of
Robert Marjolin

Edited by
RICHARD O'BRIEN

PUBLISHED BY OXFORD UNIVERSITY PRESS

For The AMEX Bank Review

1992

Oxford University Press, Walton Street, Oxford OX2 6DP
Oxford New York Toronto
Delhi Bombay Calcutta Madras Karachi
Kuala Lumpur Singapore Hong Kong Tokyo
Nairobi Dar es Salaam Cape Town
Melbourne Auckland Madrid
and associated companies in
Berlin Ibadan

Oxford is a trade mark of Oxford University Press

Published in the United States
by Oxford University Press Inc., New York

© Oxford University Press 1992

British Library Cataloguing in Publication Data
Data available

Library of Congress Cataloging in Publication Data
ISBN 0-19-828796-8

Set by Hope Services (Abingdon)Ltd.
Printed in Great Britain by
Biddles Ltd., Guildford and King's Lynn

The AMEX Bank Review Awards
In Memory of Robert Marjolin

The AMEX Bank Review Awards, launched in 1987 to promote new writing and analysis on current international economic and financial issues, are given annually in memory of Professor Robert Marjolin, the first head of the OECD (at that time the OEEC) and Vice-President of the European Commission for the first ten years of the European Community's existence. Professor Marjolin was one of the key architects of the Community and instrumental in establishing international economic cooperation in the post-war period. From 1975 to 1986 he was Editorial Adviser to *The AMEX Bank Review*: his wise and friendly advice was a constant encouragement in attempting to interpret current economic events.

Robert Marjolin was one of the most distinguished European economists and public servants of his generation. He was a very practically minded economist, being more interested in achieving progress than advocating any one particular economic theory or dogma. In 1989 the English language edition of Robert Marjolin's memoirs, under the title *Robert Marjolin: Architect of European Unity* was published by Weidenfeld and Nicolson and provides important insights into the integration process in Europe. As *The Economist* wrote in its review of these memoirs,

Robert Marjolin is a name that will ring bells in many people's minds but come into focus in few of them. Intellectually too honest either to be a forceful politician or to have the unreasonable convictions that take men to fame, he remained an *eminence grise* in postwar Europe.

The Awards are judged by a special committee of bankers, economists and politicians, which in 1992 included: *Professor Raymond Barre*, former Prime Minister of France and former Vice President of the European Commission (and Robert Marjolin's successor at the Commission); *Karl Otto Pöhl*, Partner, Sal Oppenheim jr & Cie, and former President of the Deutsche Bundesbank (and former Chairman of the EC Central Bank Governors' Committee, first established in 1964 on the recommendation of Robert Marjolin); *Lord Roll of Ipsden*, President of S. G. Warburg Group plc; *Toyoo Gyohten*, Chairman, Bank of Tokyo Ltd and former Vice Minister of Finance for International Affairs, Japan; *John Flemming*, Chief Economist, European Bank for Reconstruction & Development; *Professor Rudiger Dornbusch*, Massachusetts Institute of Technology, USA; *Rupert Pennant-Rea*, Editor, The Economist; *Bruce MacLaury*, President of the Brookings Institution, Washington DC; *Kevin Pakenham*, Chief Executive of the London investment group, John Govett & Co. Limited; and *Richard O'Brien*, Chief Economist of American Express Bank Ltd. and Editor of the *Review*. Both Mr MacLaury and Mr Pakenham are Editorial Advisers to the *Review*. The Bank is most grateful for the major contribution of the committee members in judging this competition.

The 1992 Competition

The year 1992 was the sixth year of the competition, and a record number of 301 entries were received from a total of 65 countries. As in previous years, essays were on any subject in international economics of current relevance to financial markets.

Eleven prizes were awarded, of a total value of US$56,000. The awards for the first three essays were US$25,000, US$10,000 and US$5,000 respectively, with eight Special Merit Awards of US$2,000. Summaries of all essays are published in the November 1992 issue of *The AMEX Bank Review*.

The 1992 results were announced at a special presentation dinner at the Grosvenor House Hotel, London, on 9th November 1992. The awards were presented by John Flemming, Chief Economist of the EBRD and member of the Awards Committee. His speech, marking the third anniversary of the fall of the Berlin Wall, will be published in the December 1992 issue of the *Review*. The dinner was presided over by Steven Goldstein, President and Chief Executive Officer of American Express Bank Ltd. Previous guest presenters have included former European Commissioner Lord Cockfield, the Governor of the Bank of England, the Rt. Hon. Robin Leigh-Pemberton and Awards judges Professor Raymond Barre, Karl Otto Pöhl, and Toyoo Gyohten.

The Editors
The AMEX Bank Review

Contents

viii   *Contents*

Editor's Introduction

This book contains the full texts of the eleven prize-winning essays in *The 1992 AMEX Bank Review* Awards, the essay competition run by American Express Bank Ltd. in memory of Professor Robert Marjolin. The *Review* is the monthly international economics and financial publication of the Bank and is published from London.

The 1992 collection begins with a group of four essays, headed by the first prize essay, which all focus on the economic and financial challenges facing countries in East/Central Europe and the former Soviet Union; the rest of the collection covers a diverse range of subjects (the essay competition has no set subject).

The first prize essay, by Professor Richard Rose, calls for the encouragement of a 'civil' economy in Eastern Europe, to avoid criminalising economic activities by imposing taxes that cannot be collected, and to concentrate on establishing effective 'second-best' tax handles. The next two essays in this group examine first, the role of incentives and planning in the economic transformation of former planned economies and secondly, enterprise reform in Eastern Europe. The fourth essay in this group, after tracing the experience of the dissolution of the Habsburg Empire, proposes an IMF-led scheme, including a temporary payments union, to combat the disintegration of trade in the former Soviet Union.

The rest of the collection starts with the second prize essay on financial market regulation, which concludes that while regulations may be harmonised across borders for purposes of combating systemic risk and promoting market efficiency, harmonisation is not appropriate with respect to promoting fairness. The third prize essay, by economists at the Banca d'Italia, compares the EC and the USA as optimal currency areas, comparing their homogeneity, the efficiency of the exchange rate instrument and the availability of budgetary tools to face asymmetric shocks. The final five essays, presented alphabetically by author, cover in turn: the environment ("Value-Added" does not Pollute); New Zealand's experience in targeting inflation, written by senior officials of the country's central bank; the informal economy in Africa; the unfinished business in completing the EC single financial market, particularly in the market for household savings, by the senior economist of the largest mutual life assurance company in the EC; and last but not least, the effect of the fall in Japanese equity prices on the attitude of Japanese companies towards the cost and use of capital.

Essay Selection

As in past years, the judges were looking for several characteristics in the essays, in particular the extent of new thinking or research, though well-written essays bringing together more familiar but complex issues continued to fare well. Authors are also called upon to draw out clear conclusions and recommendations from the analysis and to make their work 'accessible' to a wide international audience.

Although the essays are judged on an anonymous basis (therefore with no regard for rank, reputation or geography) it is pleasing to see an increasing geographical dispersion of the winners in 1992, with nationals or residents of no less than eight countries featured amongst the authors of the eleven winning essays, viz: Germany, Italy, Japan, the Netherlands, New Zealand, Nigeria, the UK and the USA, with a wide subject matter to match. This list brings to 25 the number of countries represented in the prize-winning lists since the Awards started in 1987. Once again winners come from both the public sector (central banks and multilateral finance institutions), the private sector (banking, insurance, consultancy and the law) and from the research world (academia and public policy research institutes).

Prize Winners' Forum

For the third year in succession, all prize winners have been invited to debate their ideas at a public seminar in London: as in 1991, the 1992 Prize Winners' Forum was hosted by the Royal Institute for International Affairs (Chatham House) London, on November 10th 1992.

All the essays are published in the form in which they were submitted to the competition, with only minor changes, including some updating. Short summaries and author biographies are presented with each essay. We are of course very pleased that all the essays continue to be published by Oxford University Press: cooperation by all concerned enables the work to be published only two months after final revision.

We hope that the essays will provide stimulating reading on current issues in international economics and finance and, not least, encourage the submission of a further set of high quality entries, by scholars, public officials and private sector practitioners, for the 1993 competition.

The Editor
The AMEX Bank Review

London
November 1992

Eastern Europe's Need for a Civil Economy

FIRST PRIZE

Summary

In Eastern Europe it is necessary to distinguish between legal and illegal economies as well as between market and non-market economies. The old command economy was legal but non-market; it also spawned parasitical and illegal markets. The critical question today is: Are East European societies developing a civil economy, which is legal as well as a market economy, or institutionalizing an uncivil economy outside the law? Just as a free society depends upon private markets, so a flourishing private sector depends upon the law and order of a *Rechtstaat* (a state based on right not might).

Because the official economy does not provide a sufficient income for everyday needs, the majority of East Europeans depend upon a mixture of legal, alegal and illegal economies. This can help people through the dislocations of transition, but it cannot build a modern market economy. The potential revenue loss from a flourishing uncivil economy is so great as to threaten the destabilization of fiscal systems.

To encourage the development of a civil economy, policymakers should avoid criminalizing economic activities by imposing taxes that its officials cannot collect, and making expenditure commitments as if it could administer a tax system like Scandinavia. Otherwise, taxes will generate gross inequities between enterprises and workers. This can be avoided by relying upon effective 'second best' tax handles, and making social benefits dependent upon payment of national insurance contributions.

Professor **Richard Rose** is director of the Centre for the Study of Public Policy, University of Strathclyde, and editor of the *Journal of Public Policy*. He has been a guest professor at the Central European University, Prague; the Wissenschaftszentrum Berlin; the European University Institute, Florence; Johns Hopkins University; and a visiting scholar at the International Monetary Fund, the American Enterprise Institute and the Brookings Institution, Washington DC. He has authored or edited more than three dozen books, participated in conferences and seminars in more than two dozen countries, and his writings have been translated into twelve languages. Professor Rose is a Fellow of the British Academy.

1

Eastern Europe's Need for a Civil Economy

RICHARD ROSE*

The transformation of ex-Communist societies in Eastern Europe today involves a double revolution: a political shift from totalitarianism to democracy, and a shift from a centrally planned to a market economy.

Democracy requires a civil society in which individuals, informal groups and formal institutions are free to pursue interests and ideals independently of the state. Free competitive elections show that the institutions of a civil society are beginning to emerge following the dismantling of the totalitarian apparatus of Soviet-style regimes.

The market presupposes a private sector too. Its introduction requires dismantling the controls of a command economy so that individuals and enterprises can freely buy and sell goods. But a market also requires the enforcement of laws. It is the state, not the market, that legislates property rights. It is the state, not the market, that sees that contracts are enforced. It is the state, not the market, that maintains public order, without which enterprises cannot invest with security. The privatization of an historically planned economy requires a secure framework of public law, which only the state can supply.

The existence of a *Rechtstaat* (a state based on right not might) requires both public officials *and* citizens to respect the rule of law. Yet individuals seeking freedom from oppressive rule may want to ignore obligations to pay taxes for social benefits that the state provides, and public officials accustomed to turning public office to private benefit must put their civic obligations before private advantage.

A civil economy is a precondition for the success of the market. The alternative, and uncivil economy, is a mixed economy of illegal and legal activities. Petty entrepreneurs can flourish in the shadows of an

* I am grateful to the Paul Lazarsfeld Society, Vienna, the Austrian National Bank and the Bundesministerium für Wissenschaft und Forschung for supporting surveys of seven nations that provide the empirical data reported herein, and to Dr. Ljubo Sirc, of Slovenia and Glasgow, for stimulating comments on an earlier draft.

uncivil economy, and households that shut out intrusive Communist authorities may want to shut out tax collectors of a democratically elected government.

But whatever the short-term incentives of individuals to scoff at the law, such behaviour has harmful long-term consequences. In the short term, an uncivil economy makes government an ineffectual 'broken-backed' democracy. Uncivil activities, such as running an illegal taxi service or doing household repairs without declaring earnings to the tax authorities, are usually labour-intensive services. Their rate of growth is thus lower than capital-intensive activities. But capitalists will not risk investing large sums in activities that depend upon illegality for profit. Because they have no legal title to their resources, uncivil entrepreneurs are discouraged from investing capital in large enterprises that create thousands of jobs and promote large-scale economic growth (see Dallago, 1990, chapter 8; Rose, 1992).

The attainment of sustained economic growth necessary to achieve consumption and social welfare benefits at the level of Western Europe requires a civil economy. Hence, the critical question facing Eastern Europe today is: *Are East European economics in transition moving toward a civil or an uncivil economy?*

Distinguishing Between Economies

East European governments have turned their backs on a centrally planned economy, but the course ahead is open. The development of market mechanisms to determine supply and demand is a necessary but not a sufficient condition for a civil economy. It also requires individuals and firms to respect the laws of property, contract and taxation. If this does not happen, a society will become an uncivil economy, in which markets operate without regard for law, and the state cannot collect the taxes that citizens are legally meant to pay.

The distinction between market and non-market economies is familiar. In the former the production and consumption of goods is regulated through the price system; in a non-market economy bureaucratic commands are central (Kornai, 1990). Legality is equally important in characterizing the market: is economic activity inside or outside the law? (Figure 1). To say that there is no difference between a legal and an illegal market is to be an idiot in the original Greek sense of a person indifferent to civic responsibilities.

Figure 1   A Typology of Civil and Uncivil Economies

	MARKET	
	Yes	No
LEGAL		
Yes	Civil	Command
No	Uncivil	Parasitical

Every post-Communist society is cursed with the legacy of a *command economy*. It was legal, for the constitution gave ownership and control of economic institutions to the state. It was legalistic not economistic, for central planning was undertaken by bureaucrats deciding who produced what, when and how. Plans were monitored by detailed periodic reporting. Managers in command economies became expert in exploiting connections to secure the goods and services needed to meet production targets. Because failure to meet plan targets could be labelled a political crime as well as an economic failing, managers engaged in duplicity, doctoring their accounts to make everything appear in order on paper.

Command economies spawned a parallel *parasitical economy*, lacking legality and allocating goods by coercion rather than through purchase. The so-called Moscow *mafiosi* display such behaviour today. Such brigands depend upon others producing goods and services for them to steal. Parasites also require markets to sell illegally seized goods. Thus, they can only exist if there are producers and consumers to be exploited.

The command economy could run without signals of demand and supply, but it could not run without the political power needed to replace market incentives with centralized allocation by the state. Communist regimes used their power to dispense with feedback from the marketplace as well as feedback from the ballot box. That power is no more. What is to fill the vacuum?

In Eastern Europe today the effective choice is between two different kinds of market economies. A *civil economy* is the Western norm, but the legal concepts of private property, contracts, profit and loss accounts, and joint stock companies have been absent there. The legal framework of a civil economy is consistent with an unregulated, a social democratic or a social market system. In a democracy, this choice is resolved by competitive elections.

A market can be created instantly by the non-enforcement of laws of a centrally planned economy. Street markets not only sell locally produced goods and services but also attract traders who, in the classic peddlar's mode, buy cheap and sell dear wherever this is possible, driving vans of goods from Berlin or Istanbul to Warsaw or Sofia. The law is scoffed at; bribes are paid to smuggle goods across borders and traders can literally operate on a fly-by-night basis.

A market that ignores legal obligations is an *uncivil economy*. Within an uncivil economy individuals and firms can buy and sell on terms freely accepted by both parties, as in the private sector in a market economy. Hiring a person to do a house repair is an example of this. Uncivil transactions can also involve the willing trade in illegal goods and services, such as prostitution or drugs. The uncivil economy also includes unwilling trade in services, as when mobs extort protection money or doctors, pharmacists and teachers extort 'tips' (that is, cash bribes) to provide services that by law are meant to be free of charge. A positivist can ignore the breaking of laws, seeing it as a rational response to incentives, arguing: 'A market is a market is a market'.

So accustomed are economists to operating within a framework of a lawful society where corporate and national income accounts both have integrity that they mistakenly assume that the collapse of a command economy automatically creates a civil economy. This is shown in the use of official statistics produced by the planning apparatus of the old regime, notwithstanding their distortion of quantities, qualities and money values: 'To get accustomed to 'small' frauds is like economic narcotics. It quickly leads to the decay of management and deception on a large scale' (quoted in Aslund, 1990:19; see also OECD, 1991).

East European societies today have a mixed economy, but the mix is different than in OECD nations; it is a mixture of civil *and* uncivil elements. The dismantling of the command economy makes it imperative to encourage economic activity independent of the state, yet a civil economy will only come into being if individuals as employees and employers and as producers and consumers accept the obligations as well as the privileges that constitute behaviour in a civil economy.

Getting By With a Multiplicity of Economies

Ordinary people in Eastern Europe today face an existential problem: *What to do in the long interval between the collapse of a centrally planned economy and the achievement of a market economy*? Mass behaviour is critical, for a market will only become civilized if the great majority of employers, workers and traders routinely comply with laws of property, contract and taxation.

Everyone socialized into an East European society has had to learn how to manage a portfolio of economies, some legal and some illegal; some monetized and some involving production without money. Factory managers responsible for meeting plan quotas have had to barter, bribe and engage in autarkic production of supplies. Some of the activities that individuals engage in to supplement their official income have positive features (home-grown food) but others are undesirable (paying bribes to doctors and nurses for health care). In centrally planned economies, most families routinely engage in both civil and uncivil behaviour (cf. Table 1).

Only the *official economy* is a civil economy. It is civil because employers and employees are legally recognized and expected to obey laws. Yet it is not a market economy as long as official enterprises are

Table 1 Participation in Seven Economies

	Mean	BUL	CS	HU	POL	ROM
			(% participating)			
OFFICIAL economy: legal, monetized						
1. Member of household in Official Economy	68	60	76	69	58	78
SOCIAL economies: non-monetized, alegal						
2. Household production	89	94	91	81	75	95
3. Help friends and relatives	59	76	53	60	49	56
4. Uses, is used as connection free	47	70	33	37	48	48
UNCIVIL economies: illegal, monetized						
5. Householder member in Second Economy	19	10	25	21	17	21
6. Pays, is paid as connection	32	30	13	17	38	60
7. Uses foreign currency	12	9	12	9	15	17

Source: Nationwide representative surveys in Bulgaria, Czechoslovakia, Hungary, Poland and Romania, as reported in Paul Lazarsfeld Gesellschaft, (1992)

funded as public agencies, prices do not reflect laws of supply and demand, and firms can continue operating when by market standards they would be bankrupt. Even though most households in Eastern Europe have at least two people working in the official economy, only one-third report that their earnings are adequate to buy the things that the family needs. In the words of a Bulgarian proverb, 'If you have to live from one job, you will die'. To help meet their household needs, people turn to a variety of other economies.

Three *social economies* are alegal, lacking official authorization and recognition. As markets they are unusual because they operate without money; family and friendship ties are the basis of exchange.

The household functions as an economy in the original Greek sense of the word. More than seven-eighths of households in Eastern Europe spend a substantial amount of time growing their own food, repairing or building their house, or queuing for more than an hour a day to buy food and households goods that are chronically in short supply. Exchanging goods and services among friends and relatives is important in more than half of households. Whereas in a Western society giving a ride in a car to a person who also has a car is a social activity, in Eastern Europe a person with a car may drive a friend without a car to his vegetable plot to produce food for their mutual benefit. When a connection is needed for something, nearly half of households can get what they need through friends of friends without paying a bribe.

Three economies are *uncivil*; they are monetized, but participants scoff at civic obligations. Because the private sector was not legal in a centrally planned economy, a second job is regarded as part of the unofficial second economy. Typically, it is a one-day-a-week job different from a person's official occupation; no taxes are paid and no social security benefits are earned. Only one in five reports a second job. This is not evidence of a disinclination to work in the second economy but because effective demand is lacking. People only work in the second economy if they are paid cash in hand, and most East Europeans do not have a lot of cash for such purposes.

Tips or bribes paid to connections are not only illegal but also anti-social. Public officials exploit their position to ask for payments on the side to do what they are supposed to do without a bribe. East Europeans often must pay a bribe to use nominally free state social services such as hospital treatment, and side-payments for consumer goods can substitute for the market economy's reliance upon allocation by price.

Dealing in foreign currency is a vote of no confidence in government, denying that there is any value in the nation's currency. Foreigners making payments in dollars in an East European capital city are not dealing with a cross-section of the population. It is hard for factory workers or people in provincial towns and villages to meet people who have dollars; only one-eighth of households sometimes deal in foreign currency.

After four decades of living with the shortages of planned economies, almost two-thirds of East Europeans have learned how to combine resources from two or more economies in order to get by, that is, maintain themselves without drawing on their savings or borrowing. The average household is active in at least three different economies. But just as investors differ in their portfolios, so ordinary families differ in the way in which they combine resources from different economies (see Rose and Haerpfer, 1992: 11ff).

Half the households follow a defensive strategy; to survive in a turbulent economic environment they retreat from the money economy to a pre-modern economy, growing food, relying upon do-it-yourself activities, and exchanges with friends, relatives, and friends of friends. Going on the defensive makes sense for households worried about the uncertainties of economic change, but it contributes nothing to the positive development of a modern economy.

More than a quarter believe that two money incomes are better than one. Enterprising households rely to an important extent upon earnings from an uncivil economy as well as upon a job in the official economy. For the majority of enterprising families, the money earned in an uncivil economy is secondary to work in the official economy. But if the latter turns sour, they can commit more effort to earning money in ways outside the cognizance of official statistics.

Everyone in a society in transformation is vulnerable to the pervasive impact of change. The most vulnerable are not the poorest members of society but those who have previously relied solely upon the official economy for work or a pension. Often, vulnerable people are relatively well paid, for example, leading workers in factories or civil servants in ministries. Vulnerable people have no uncivil alternative to turn to if the enterprises that employ them collapse under the pressures of the market. This group contrasts with the tenth of the population that is marginal, living without any significant cash income, for example, elderly people in the countryside who since childhood have endured poverty, war, and totalitarianism.

The tactics that individuals use to cope with economies in transition are rational in the short term. But what may make short-term sense for individuals can contradict long-term goals. As long as households concentrate their efforts on household production they will never be able to enjoy those things that money can buy, such as a car, a modern house, or a colour television. The 'creative destruction' of the old system provides new opportunities for people to earn money in uncivil economies (cf. Sik, 1992). But as long as individuals concentrate on earning money illegally, they will always be vulnerable to arrest, blackmail or coercion, and they have no claim to social benefits, such as health care, unemployment benefits or a pension in old age.

Even though Lawrence Summers (1992:29) is correct in stating that 'growth in the informal sector is almost surely understated in our statistics', the inference that he draws—'the numbers paint a much darker picture than is warranted'—is only true of the short term. Substantial activity outside the official economy distorts the economy and is an obstacle to investment in long-term growth. Those who get rich from uncivil enterprises are more likely to engage in conspicuous consumption, buying foreign cars and jewellery, rather than saving. Foreign banks will not want to loan money to individuals and activities in violation of the law. Foreign firms will not invest money in enterprises that depend upon 'off the books' activities for profits. Short-term material benefits of uncivil economies cannot provide the foundation for the sustained economic growth needed to bring Eastern Europeans up to the standard of living of Western Europeans.

Implications For Tax Policy

In political terms the revolution in Eastern Europe is a liberal revolution, intended to reduce the influence of government, but it is not an anarchic rejection of all government. The new economic order is meant to be a civil order, in which the state guarantees the rule of law necessary for private enterprises to develop, and private enterprises respect their legal obligation to pay taxes financing education, health care, and social protection for individuals pushed below subsistence level by the transition to the market economy.

Governments in Eastern Europe now face a big fiscal squeeze because they have inherited large spending commitments without the money to finance them (OECD, 1991a). Centrally planned economies did not need to worry about taxation. Government took its cut from the flow of funds before they ever reached the hands of individuals, and one-party regimes had no fear of election defeat.

The revenue-raising practices of the command economy are no longer viable. East European governments are introducing Western-style tax systems which assume a stable and buoyant source of tax revenue from economic activity in the official economy. But the deconstruction of the official economy will inevitably reduce the size of easily collected tax revenue, as growth occurs primarily in the uncivil economy and the substitution of non-monetized work for taxable activities. East European governments thus risk a big shortfall in revenue.

Ironically, stabilization programmes may lead to the destabilization of economies in transition. Privatization through the sale of large enterprises in the official economy and demobilizing non-productive employees in the official sector increase the number working in hard-to-tax economies. The 'new' private sector is an inexperienced in paying taxes as the state is in collecting them. Governments will thus experience a big shortfall in revenue. The losses in tax revenue are likely to be much greater than domestically chosen or internationally mandated reductions in public expenditure, and notional cuts may be offset by pressures to increase spending on the unemployed and on infrastructure improvements. The widening gap between public revenue and expenditure will inflate economies which already have too much inflation, and reduce confidence in government institutions that have yet to establish a reputation for effectiveness.

Eastern Europe's governors do not have the leisure to debate the question, 'How much ought government to levy in taxes?' The practical question is: 'How much can the government actually collect?' One of the oldest maxims of taxation is that you can't spend what you cannot collect. If a government violates this rule by turning to the printing presses to finance its expenditure, the resulting inflation debases its political as well as its financial authority.

Every East European government has a material as well as a moral incentive to promote the development of the civil economy. What can policymakers do?

The first injunction is negative: *avoid criminalization*. Tax policy encourages criminalization when laws provide big incentives for individuals and enterprises to channel activities into uncivil economies.

For example, a highly progressive income tax encourages big money-makers to turn to the uncivil economy, keeping their earnings in foreign bank accounts. Enacting laws that assume that a modern, civil economy already exists can have the unintended consequence of increasing criminalization. Newly industrializing economies are better models for East European tax systems than contemporary Scandinavian welfare states. Newly industrializing nations have a large rural sector, significant alegal or illegal economies, no tradition of routine tax payment, and few institutions effectively collecting taxes.

A second priority is: *avoid overcommitment on expenditure*. This prescription is not derived from timeless neo-liberal injunctions against public expenditure but from prudential public finance norms about the need to limit deficits. Unexpectedly large deficits can occur even in countries with effective tax systems; the likelihood is far greater where the tax system is untested. To budget for big-spending social programmes on the grounds that 100 per cent of taxes lawfully due can be collected by inexperienced tax officials is unrealistic in the extreme. It will exacerbate inflation, for the spending commitments will be binding, but many tax bills will not be paid.

Keeping a tight hand on social expenditure will not produce the negative welfare effects that would be inferred from statistics about the official economy. If its figures were taken literally, then almost everybody in an Eastern European society would be classified as necessitous, with incomes as low as $10 or $20 a week. But such figures should not be taken literally, since most East European households have a portfolio of economies that enable them to get by, and this is true even of marginal households (Rose, forthcoming). One member losing a job will not deprive a household of all its money income but only reduce it by a fraction, and allow more time for do-it-yourself household production or seeking income in uncivil economies. The great majority likely to become unemployed are suitable candidates for vocational training for they are relatively young, urban and educated.

Avoid major inequities between enterprises is a third rule for civilizing the economy. Public agencies cannot avoid paying social security taxes or withholding income tax. Large enterprises, especially those with foreign investment, are politically visible and their need for bureaucratized accounting procedures forces them to pay many taxes. By contrast, small family enterprises, farmers and the self-employed can operate on a cash basis facilitating tax evasion. If there is universal entitlement to social benefits, then 100 per cent of households will enjoy benefits that must be financed by taxes that effectively cover little more than half the labour force.

Relating social benefits to contributions will teach citizens that in public policy as in the marketplace every benefit has a cost. An earmarked tax for health care will make people realize that even if a health service is free of charge at the point of delivery, it is not produced free of cost. If people of working age are entitled to publicly financed health services only if they can prove payment to the health fund, then those who do not pay do not benefit, and evaders concerned about their health have an incentive to become taxpayers. Unemployment benefits could be restricted to those who have contributed to an unemployment fund rather than made universal. This is how such systems originated in Europe and the United States. Employers forced to pay social security contributions could use its benefits to justify lower take-home pay than in uncivil firms that did not pay taxes and left their employees without social protection.

Finding effective tax handles is the immediate priority for revenue-raising. Even if a tax is in 'sub-optimal' in economic theory, if it is unavoidable in practice, this is a recommendation to governments strapped for revenue. Effective tax handles make firms and individuals law-abiding economic actors whether they will it or not (Goode, 1984). A property tax is far easier to collect than a profits tax, and it can be levied on firms as well as households. Sumptuary taxes on cars are difficult to avoid because cars can only be used on public roads. Petrol taxes can be collected at refineries and do not burden the poor, because less than half of households own cars in Eastern Europe. The maintenance of a state tobacco monopoly makes it possible to collect public revenue from smokers.

It is self-defeating to expect East European governments to achieve a civil economy overnight. Transition is a process that is likely to take a decade or more. Yet it is a process that can achieve its desired goals. Notwithstanding a long history of tax evasion, countries such as Italy and France today finance social benefits at higher levels than the United States because officials have gradually evolved a tax system consistent with a civil economy. It would be a tragic mistake if East European governments, in their rush to emulate Western practices, adopted inconsistent taxing and spending policies that undermined the achievement of a democratic political system with a civil society and a civil economy.

References

Aslund, Anders, 1990. 'How Small Is the Soviet Economy?' In Henry S. Rowen and Charles Wolf Jr., *The Impoverished Superpower*. San Francisco: ICS Press, 13–61.

Dallago, Bruno, 1990. *The Irregular Economy: the Underground Economy and the Black Labour Market*. Aldershot: Dartmouth.

Goode, Richard, 1944. *Government Finance in Developing Countries*. Washington DC: Brookings Institution.

Kornai, Janos, 1990. *Vision and Reality, Market and State*. Hemel Hempstead: Harvester Wheatsheaf.

OECD, 1991. *Statistics for a Market Economy*. Paris: OECD.

OECD, 1991a. *The Role of Tax Reform in Central and Eastern European Economies*. Paris: OECD.

Paul Lazarsfeld Gesellschaft, 1992. *Neue Demokratien Barometer*. Vienna: Paul Lazarsfeld Gesellschaft.

Rose, Richard, 1992. 'Divisions and Contradictions in Economies in Transition'. Washington DC: Report to the World Bank.

Rose, Richard, forthcoming. 'Who Needs Social Protection in Eastern Europe? A Constrained Empirical Analysis of Romania'. In Stein Ringen and Claire Wallace, eds., *Social Responses to Transformation in Eastern Europe*. Prague: Central European University Press.

Rose, Richard and Haerpfer, Christian, 1992. *New Democracies Between State and Market: A Baseline Report*. Glasgow: U. of Strathclyde Studies in Public Policy No. 204.

Sik, Endre, 1992. 'From the Second to the Informal Economy'. *Journal of Public Policy*, 12,2.

Summers, Lawrence H., 1992. 'The Next Decade in Central and Eastern Europe'. In C. Clague and G. Rausser, eds., *The Emergence of Market Economies in Eastern Europe*. Cambridge, MA: Blackwell, pp. 25–34.

The Roles of Incentives and Planning in Market-Oriented Transformations

SPECIAL MERIT AWARD

Summary

This essay addresses the types of incentives that must be established before a market economy can function effectively. These incentives, which are often taken for granted in industralized market economies, are created by the structure of employment contracts, banking regulations, bankruptcy laws, payments systems, and many other pieces of 'the woodwork' that typically receive little attention in discussions of macroeconomic policy design. Unless similar incentives are firmly embedded in the new institutional infrastructure of the previously centrally planned economies that are now undertaking market-oriented transformation, it is hard to imagine how the transformation efforts can lead anywhere but to severe economic hardship (both high unemployment and high inflation) and political instability.

The essay identifies several pressure points in the transition economy where proper incentives will be crucial. Potential problems include insolvency of financial institutions, payments restrictions for international trade, capital flight, weak incentives for foreign private investment, and perhaps most important, resistance to restructuring of state enterprises.

Michael Dooley is Professor of Economics at the University of California, Santa Cruz. He has been a staff member at the Federal Reserve Board and the International Monetary Fund and has taught at the University of Texas and the University of Chicago. He is currently a Research Associate at the National Bureau of Economic Research and Director of the Group for Comparative and Economic Studies at Santa Cruz.

Dr. Dooley has published widely in the field of international finance and economic development. Recent work on economies in transition includes papers dealing with financing needs of the CIS and the organization of trade and payments among the independent States.

Peter Isard is an Advisor in the Research Department of the International Monetary Fund, where he has contributed since 1985 to research and general policy development on the international monetary system and has participated actively during the past year on an IMF team assisting the authorities of Lithuania to design an economic stabilization and reform program. From 1972 through 1985 he served primarily with the International Finance Division of the Federal Reserve Bank, and he has also had appointments at the Bank for International Settlements and at several universities. He has published articles on a wide range of macroeconomic policy issues.

2

The Roles of Incentives and Planning in Market-Oriented Transformations

MICHAEL P. DOOLEY AND PETER ISARD*

This essay addresses various types of incentives that must be established before a market economy can function effectively. It also argues that the enormous challenge of restructuring large industrial enterprises or reabsorbing their workers, while appropriately based on market signals, cannot be accomplished by the market alone.

Incentives to Manage Scarce Resources Appropriately

The distinguishing feature of a market economy is its reliance on a system of uncontrolled prices to coordinate the behaviour of many separate economic units. Relative prices are free to adjust as necessary to equilibrate supplies and demands, and the information they convey provides an efficient guide for production and investment decisions.[1]

The benefits of a market price system will not be realized, however, if economic units lack adequate incentives to rely on relative prices. Unless decision makers perceive that reliance on relative prices can be expected to increase their individual standards of living the price adjustment mechanism will not function appropriately, and scarce resources will not be allocated efficiently.

One key area where appropriate incentives must be established is in the management of enterprises during the period before privatization. Historically, state enterprises have operated with 'soft budget constraints',[2] under which financial losses have been routinely covered or disguised with subsidies, tax concessions, or credits from the state. To break the mentality of soft budget constraints, and to establish financial

* The views expressed in this essay are those of the authors and do not necessarily represent the views of the International Monetary Fund.

discipline based on market prices, 'employment contracts' must be established that link the remuneration of managers and workers elastically to financial performance.[3] Managers and workers must perceive that they face significant losses if they ignore the information provided by relative prices.[4] At the same time, to maintain popular support for the transformation process, macroeconomic reform programmes must make it feasible for managers and workers, acting in response to market signals, to avoid sharp declines in living standards in the short run and to raise their living standards over time. Successful behavioural modification requires that bad performers incur losses, but also that most participants in the economy have incentives to support an ongoing transformation process.

Conditions for Credit Allocation Mechanisms to Function Effectively

Another key area in which appropriate incentive structures are crucial is in the operation of credit allocation mechanisms. A well known economic theorist has concluded that capital markets are like bumble bees. Engineers can prove that bumble bees do not meet the minimum requirements for flight. Finance experts can show that financial markets do not provide the minimum level of information and trust required for savers to set their wealth adrift in a capital market.

Bumble bees do fly and capital markets in a few industrial countries do work most of the time. But trying to transplant modern capital markets into developing countries has proven exceedingly difficult. Furthermore, trying to control the growth of money and credit with tools that work in a few industrial countries can lead to very poor macroeconomic performance.

The fundamental precondition for credit markets to function effectively is so basic it seems trivial. It is that at *every* point of a chain of financial intermediation there must be strong incentives for participants to satisfy their contractual obligations, even when doing so incurs losses. In the absence of effective nonfinancial punishment mechanisms, performance is only assured if each participant has a positive net worth that a counterparty can appropriate as a penalty for nonperformance. Moreover, counterparties must be able to monitor both the assets of participants and other claims on those assets.

Participants in credit markets often invest in reputation in order to maintain the trust of others. But recent experience in industrial countries emphasizes that any hole in a system of accountability attracts individuals for whom reputation is less important than a fast dollar. Thus, accountability requires in practice that each position-taker in the capital markets maintain a positive net worth.

This criterion is not met in an economy in transition. Inevitably, the large relative price changes associated with moving toward a market economy will make many existing firms insolvent. Moreover, banks and other firms will inherit stocks of worthless claims on the insolvent firms.[5]

It is hard to imagine conditions that create a worse incentive structure for a private capital market. Insolvent firms have every incentive to cover operating losses by borrowing from banks, while banks that are already insolvent have nothing to lose by carrying insolvent firms with new credit. Moreover, new credit allows banks to carry old loans to insolvent firms at full value.

The establishment of an appropriate incentive structure requires financial restructuring, and delaying actions to clean up the balance sheets of banks and nonbank state enterprises can have costly consequences. In particular, market-oriented monetary control mechanisms will not curb the inflationary growth of money and credit in a situation with insolvent firms. Suppose, for example, that the authorities attempt to restrict the growth of credit by maintaining positive and, by historical standards, high real interest rates on bank credit. A natural reaction of solvent firms will be to withdraw from credit markets. Insolvent firms will be less intimidated. In fact, at very high real rates only insolvent firms will apply to banks for additional credit. In this extreme case the banking system is implicitly insured by the government. Raising interest rates further may actually increase the rate of monetary expansion. The only way to stop this process is for the government to administratively exclude the insolvent firms and banks from the credit markets. The irony of this argument should be evident. Although we have great respect for the power of markets to help countries in transition join the rest of the world in the benefits of market-oriented institutions, we see great danger in overlooking the nonmarket institutional structure upon which markets depend.

These perspectives underscore the importance of cleaning up the balance sheets of banks and nonbank state enterprises at an early stage in the transformation process, and of somehow insuring that all intermediaries and ultimate borrowers in domestic financial markets have something to lose. In some cases the latter objective can be achieved by endowing intermediaries and ultimate borrowers with equalization claims on the public sector in connection with a monetary reform process.[6]

The above considerations also point to the danger of rationing credit on the basis of interest rates alone. Avoiding a high incidence of default requires a careful ex ante evaluation of prospective borrowers, which in turn requires access to meaningful information about their balance sheets and cash flow prospects. Accordingly, while indirect control over market interest rates can be relied upon to drive away some credit applicants,[7] interest rates should only be pushed up to a level that still leaves a reasonably large excess demand for credit, thereby providing adequate scope for screening out high risk borrowers via creditworthiness evaluations.

Incentives to Accept Financial Payments for Goods and Services

The former centrally-planned economies are launching their market-oriented transformation efforts with highly-specialized industrial structures, and are heavily dependent on each other as sources of inputs and markets for output. The specific physical characteristics of intermediate products, as well as quality characteristics, limit the extent to which producers can shift in the short run to new sources of inputs, or find new markets for outputs. In this context, a significant part of the output losses of the former CMEA countries since the beginning of 1991 has been associated with a curtailment of purchases by the former Soviet Union (FSU). Similarly, the progressive disruption of trade during 1991–92 among the individual republics of the FSU has led to widespread production cutbacks.

The drying up of trade among republics of the FSU appears to be largely associated with shortages of hard currency reserves and the lack of a workable financial payments mechanism that is not heavily dependent on hard currency. Barter transactions continue to take place when they can be arranged and non-barter trade was to some extent sustained through mid-1992 by the system of correspondent accounts and the accumulation of arrears, but the era of automatic trade credit appears to have ended.

This problem needs to be addressed with urgency if recent output losses in the FSU are to be reversed and a deeper output collapse averted. Enterprises throughout the FSU need recourse to a payments instrument—either pieces of paper or accounting entries, guaranteed by a credible institution, and backed with hard currency—that they can use to purchase imports from other republics, and that they are willing to accept in payment for exports. A net settlements mechanism (perhaps, but not necessarily, involving a formal payments union) could greatly economize on the amount of hard currency that would actually be required for settlements, but only if enterprises are willing to accept the payment guarantees of whatever institution stands behind the system.

In market economies where there is general confidence in private financial institutions, international payments are often made with bankers' acceptances. The exporter is willing to accept payment from an importer when a reputable bank guarantees that it will deliver funds for the importer.

By contrast, there currently appears to be no private or government institution within the FSU whose payment guarantees are widely acceptable in other countries. One possible solution to the problem would be for each of the 'countries' involved to deposit hard currency (or gold) reserves with some reputable outside official institution (such as the Bank for International Settlements), which would then perform the necessary clearinghouse functions. If appropriate, the initial reserves could come in part from official external assistance flows, and quantitative floors could be set on reserve holdings within the clearing-house as part of the conditionality governing subsequent external credit flows.

For such a settlements mechanism to operate effectively, however, all parties would have to have strong incentives to meet their settlement obligations. If national governments accept responsibility for standing behind the settlement obligations of enterprises residing in their countries, it is important that monitoring procedures be in place to control the import activities of large enterprises that remain subject to soft budget constraints. Indeed, because private entrepreneurs will be quick to recognize opportunities for state enterprises to evade controls by exploiting opportunities to import or conduct other restricted activities through private intermediaries, an economy-wide system of monitoring import documents may be strongly advisable to help maintain overall balance between imports and exports during the period until large state enterprises have been privatized. There must also be an enforceable mechanism for penalizing any national governments that do not meet their settlement obligations.

Incentives for Residents to Hold Domestic Financial Assets

The viability of any macroeconomic reform effort depends critically on its success in attracting resources to finance productive investment. Accordingly, the authorities must attempt to create strong incentives for residents to increase their holdings of domestic financial assets and for non-residents to provide capital inflows.

In an economy in which domestic residents have been effectively prevented from moving savings abroad, the removal or relaxation of restrictions on international transactions may lead to large-scale capital outflows, even in the presence of sound monetary and fiscal policies. Capital outflows in this context would simply represent a rational attempt to diversify sources of income by residents who initially are totally reliant on domestic labour and capital income. Diversification reduces the extent to which total income is exposed to any one particular type of risk. Thus, even if the expected returns on domestic assets were somewhat higher than those on foreign assets, the portfolio diversification motive could provide strong incentives for residents to reduce their exposure to shocks affecting domestic incomes and increase their exposure to shocks affecting foreign incomes.

The domestic authorities basically have two ways they can attempt to prevent large-scale capital outflows. One approach is to enhance the attractiveness of domestic financial assets—both by acting to instil confidence in the financial institutions that provide domestic savings vehicles, and by implementing macroeconomic policies that are conducive to high yields on domestic investments. The second approach is to rely on capital controls.

Controls on capital outflows can be justified under two conditions: when the country does not have access to offsetting capital inflows; and when net capital outflows generate negative externalities. Both conditions seem realistic for the countries pursuing market-oriented transformations. To the extent that the success of a transformation effort depends critically on the strength of domestic investment, individual decisions to move capital abroad generate negative externalities, and the residents of a country undertaking reforms may well be better off individually when they are collectively forced to keep capital at home than when each freely chooses to move capital abroad. Capital controls can thus be justified as the solution to a coordination problem in the presence of the negative externalities.

Whether capital controls are effective is quite another matter. A number of countries have experienced large scale capital flight in the presence of controls. Obviously, the strength of the incentive to move capital abroad in the presence of controls depends on the size of the prospective gains from doing so, on the ability to do so without being detected, and on the costs of being detected.

The prospective gains from moving capital out of a country obviously depend on the attractiveness of the country's macroeconomic prospects. Unless residents have confidence in the country's policy institutions and policy stances, and unless the country has adequate international liquidity and faces a favourable external environment, it may be difficult for residents to resist any opportunities they have to move capital abroad. To some extent, however, the temptation to evade controls can be countered by imposing severe penalties on any residents caught doing so.

The ability of residents to evade capital controls will generally depend on arrangements governing convertibility for current account transactions. Indeed, many countries that claim to have established current account convertibility have actually retained various exchange restrictions on current account transactions, implicitly recognizing the dangers of capital outflows through the current account. Countries that document exports and impose foreign exchange surrender or repatriation requirements on exporters, and that require those who bid for foreign exchange to provide documents of import orders or other bona fide current account transactions, may be able to monitor current account transactions fairly closely, thereby making it easier to detect attempts to move capital out of the country. Needless to say, careful consideration should be given to devising a mechanism that minimizes the bureaucratic hassles and administrative costs of filing documents and obtaining foreign exchange, and that keeps the market for foreign exchange competitive.

One approach that may be attractive is to make it illegal for residents to hold foreign exchange per se, but to establish an unrestrictive competitive and unified market for foreign exchange certificates, and to allow importers to convert these certificates automatically (at a fixed 1:1 conversion rate) into foreign exchange when import documents are approved. At the same time, exporters and recipients of transfers or capital inflows would be required to surrender their foreign exchange receipts for foreign exchange certificates that they could either retain, deposit in interest bearing accounts, or sell.[8][9] Under such a system, the domestic currency price of foreign exchange certificates would essentially represent the exchange rate between domestic and foreign currencies, and the domestic authorities would have the option of orienting their monetary policy toward stabilizing this exchange rate if they so desired.

The threat of capital flight underscores the importance of strong and credible transformation programmes. It also suggests that, where external resources are meagre and macroeconomic prospects are subject to a high degree of uncertainty, a cautious approach to convertibility is advisable.[10] The main benefits of current account convertibility come from the effects of import competition on the efficiency of domestic production and the guidance that relative prices on world markets can provide for the allocation of resources. To a large extent, countries can secure these benefits by establishing a single exchange rate for permissible transactions, removing quantitative restrictions on imports, and adopting a uniform import tariff.[11] The complete removal of all exchange restrictions relating to current account transactions is not necessary, however, to promote a healthy degree of import competition and to align internal relative prices with those on world markets. Without some exchange control mechanism or reporting system for commercial transactions, it is likely to be easy for residents to move capital out of the country through false invoicing or leads and lags in current account payments.

Incentives for Non-residents to Provide Capital Inflows

Inflows of foreign investment capital can significantly help the transformation process. When foreign investors assume ownership positions in domestic enterprises, capital inflows can also lead to new and possibly better management, and to valuable information about production technologies and marketing opportunities abroad.

Attracting foreign investment capital will be difficult, however, until a legal code is in place that clearly defines the investor's share of whatever income stream results from the investment. Uncertainty about property rights is bad for all investors, but it is particularly problematic for non-residents who could in the future provide an attractive target for domestic interest groups.

Uncertainty about macroeconomic prospects and the revenue needs of the government also creates uncertainty about effective after-tax earnings prospects, which discourages investment. And non-resident investors are likely to be particularly discouraged by uncertainty about effective tax rates since non-residents have less voice in the domestic political process.

One way to improve the climate for capital inflows is to act to reduce sources of prospective strains on future fiscal budgets, thereby reducing fears of higher effective tax rates on capital income. In this connection, debt relief can play an important role in reducing fiscal strains.

The climate for direct investment inflows also depends on the attitude of the industrialized countries toward opening their markets to imports from the transforming economies. A clear invitation for these countries to eventually join the European Community, and a commitment by the EC to keep trade barriers low in the interim, could significantly stimulate foreign direct investment flows into export-oriented activities.

Restructuring Large Enterprises and the Case for a Planning Agency

Large shares of the populations in former centrally-planned economies are employed in large industrial enterprises, many of which provide housing, health care, and other benefits in addition to wages. The mobility of the workforce is generally low, reflecting in part the lack of much available housing. Accordingly, closing a large industrial enterprise creates pressures for the government to provide income support.

Continuing to operate an industrial enterprise may also drain the government budget. Many enterprises may be generating less value added (at market prices) than the wages and other benefits they provide their employees. Some may even be generating negative value added.

The existence of large groups of essentially immobile human resources with ongoing consumption needs and desires to increase their living standards over time poses an enormous challenge. Allowing the market to simply drive these resources into unemployment is not likely to be socially acceptable; and political leaders who fail to recognize this are unlikely to survive in a democratic political system. Decisions must somehow be made about how best to re-employ human resources, taking into account their initial skills and whatever plant, equipment, and other nonhuman resources are available. In most cases, the process of changing production activities will require outlays in new equipment and material inventories, which may well require an extension of credit.

Re-employing the human resources associated with large industrial enterprises is likely to take time. In the interim, the fiscal authorities will have to spend money, both to keep people subsisting and to provide investment finance. The way in which the government divides its spending between consumption subsidies and credit to support restructuring efforts may make no difference in terms of the overall fiscal strains on its current-period budget. But it can have a major influence in shaping the incentives that motivate workers and managers, with important feedback effects on fiscal spending needs over time.

There seems to be no attractive alternative to government involvement in credit allocation—either directly or indirectly through close monitoring of state-owned banks—to finance the initial investments and other start-up costs of new activities. Private intermediaries are unlikely to be able to attract household deposits or other types of private domestic funds without government guarantees, and inflows of private foreign capital are unlikely to be forthcoming on a sufficiently large scale. Moreover, in the absence of government credit, restructuring will never occur, much of the population will remain heavily dependent on disguised or overt income support payments, and standards of living will never rise.

The government's effectiveness in providing credit for industrial restructuring will depend critically on its ability to decide what restructuring plans deserve financial support. It cannot hope to be effective in this area without acquiring considerable expertise (or outside technical advice) on production technologies, marketing issues, and other aspects of managing industrial enterprises. While much of the planning for industrial restructuring should take place at the enterprise level, there is a clear need for transitional guidance from the government.

The idea of guidance or transitional planning elicits unpleasant memories of the ineffective role that planning agencies have historically played in command economies. We are not, however, advocating a suppression of market forces or a return to the past. Nor are we advocating that the focus of planning extend beyond the large state enterprise sector; in many respects, the proper role of government is to 'get out of the way' of private entrepreneurship. Rather, the case for government intervention is based on the fact that, until the large state enterprise sector is successfully transformed or its labour force reabsorbed elsewhere, long-lasting macroeconomic stabilization will be very difficult to achieve in a democratic political system, and major costs will be incurred by other sectors of the economy.

A transitional planning agency could play important roles in exploiting economies of scale in obtaining information about production technologies and marketing opportunities, in generally providing helpful education and advice to enterprises, in monitoring enterprises to protect against 'asset stripping' or other undesirable actions in the context of a legal framework for 'corporatization' during the period prior to privatization, and in insuring that economy-wide industrial restructuring proceeds in a balanced manner.

Conclusion

This essay has argued that the transition from central planning to a market economy hinges critically on the establishment of various types of economic incentives. A successful transformation requires reforms in the structure of employment contracts, banking regulations, bankruptcy laws, payment systems, and many other pieces of 'the woodwork' that typically receive little attention in discussions of macroeconomic policy design. Without extensive structural measures to establish appropriate market incentives, it is hard to imagine how the transformation efforts can lead anywhere but to severe economic hardship (both high unemployment and high inflation) and political instability.

The essay has also argued that market mechanisms alone cannot succeed in transforming economies in which large clusters of the population are essentially immobile and initially dependent on large industrial enterprises that could not survive in a laissez-faire environment. Until these enterprises can be successfully restructured or their workers absorbed elsewhere, governments that want to maintain political support cannot avoid providing overt or disguised consumption subsidies, and durable macroeconomic stabilization will be difficult to achieve. In all likelihood, governments will also have to provide much of the credit required to restructure large industrial enterprises, and must therefore be able to evaluate restructuring prospects. Planning the transition of large industrial enterprises is unavoidable and should receive high priority from the start. Without access to considerable expertise on production technologies and marketing opportunities—whether in-house expertise or outside advice—market-oriented transformation efforts are likely to flounder.

References

Calvo, Guillermo A., and Fabrizio Coricelli, 'Stabilizing a Previously-Centrally-Planned Economy: Poland 1990', unpublished paper (January 1992).

Kornai, Janos, 'Resource-Constrained Versus Demand-Constrained Systems', *Econometrica*, Vol. 47 (July 1979), pp. 801–19.

Sachs, Jeffrey D., 'Crossing the Valley of Tears in East European Reform', *Challenge*, Vol. 34 (September/October 1991), pp. 26–34.

Notes

1 Efficient allocation requires that the relative prices faced by decentralized decision makers accurately reflect relative marginal costs and benefits to society. In the presence of monopolies, externalities, or 'noneconomic objectives', there may be a case for appropriate controls on some relative prices.
2 Kornai (1979).
3 Financial performance, of course, must be carefully measured, with appropriate valuation of inventories and other forms of capital.
4 Managers must also be prevented from exploiting their positions in undesirable ways, perhaps by placing them under the scrutiny of boards of directors or planning agencies. See Sachs (1991).
5 Interenterprise credits are extensive in these economies, perhaps more so than credits extended from banks to nonfinancial enterprises. Moreover, many of the private commercial banks that are emerging draw their capital and deposits primarily from nonfinancial firms rather than households and should thus be regarded as new mechanisms for interenterprise credit extensions—and equally as unsupervised potential sources of financial crises.
6 See Calvo and Coricelli (1992), who use the term 'debt socialization' to refer to the process in which the government 'capitalizes' various sectors of the economy.
7 Direct controls, such as interest rate ceilings, are easily circumvented.
8 The experiences with foreign exchange certificates in Taiwan in the late 1950s and Korea in the mid 1960s may be instructive in this regard,
9 Where trade with some partner countries is settled with foreign exchange while trade in others is financed initially with settlement credits (and ultimately with hard currency via a clearinghouse mechanism), there could be

unrestricted competitive markets for both foreign exchange certificates and settlement credit certificates.

10 The system of foreign exchange certificates just described would essentially establish current account convertibility, but without allowing residents to hold foreign exchange per se.

11 It may be more advisable to rely on a depreciated exchange rate, rather than a uniform tariff, to limit the general strength of import competition, since import tariffs create a bias against production for export.

Economic Aspects of Enterprise Reform in Eastern Europe

SPECIAL MERIT AWARD

Summary

Eastern Europe is not well served with straight textbook advice. The common wisdom on privatization fails to address the problems created by the diffuse ownership and control prior to privatization. Cash auctions may not efficiently match managers and capital stock because of wealth constraints. Standard advice on enterprise restructuring fails to incorporate the consequences of the sheer scale of the problem, and of the reasons why current profits are a poor guide to future profit opportunity. Finally, introducing Western style unemployment insurance, while lowering the social costs of unemployment, would almost certainly also contribute to its indefinite extension.

This paper shows how such problems can be addressed by incorporating incentive problems specific to Eastern Europe into policy design. Sometimes the resulting advice is novel and as yet untried; in some cases successful examples exist. Thus some experimentation is unavoidable. The alternative, however, is declining incomes and increasing social unrest as the consensus underlying the reforms ends.

Sweder van Wijnbergen holds a masters degree in Physics from the University of Utrecht, the Netherlands and a Ph.D. in economics from the Massachusetts Institute of Technology. At the time of writing this article, he was at the World Bank, where he was the Lead Economist for Mexico and later for Eastern Europe. He has since left the Bank to take up a professorship at the University of Amsterdam and the LSE. He has published widely in the areas of international economics and public finance, and is specifically interested in the problems of economic reform. Recent publications include 'Mexico and the Brady Plan', *Economic Policy 1991*, and 'The Political Economy of Price Reform', *The Economic Journal 1992*.

3

Economic Aspects of Enterprise Reform in Eastern Europe

SWEDER J. G. VAN WIJNBERGEN

Price de-control has eliminated queues in Eastern Europe. It has not, however, led to much more efficient resource use; the reforms necessary for production efficiency have been surprisingly difficult to introduce. Privatization drives, after initial successes in selling off shops and restaurants, have stalled. And output in State Owned Enterprises (SOEs) has collapsed across the board. As a consequence, all countries saw GDP decline by double digit numbers in the first year central planning was abandoned.

The collapse of the SOEs has complicated macroeconomic management. Governments relied mostly on SOE profits for revenue; with the decline of SOE profitability the tax base is rapidly eroding. Since introducing a modern tax system takes time, governments face the difficult choice between cutting expenditure as taxes fall, the deepening recession notwithstanding, or reigniting inflation through increasing monetization. Moreover, widespread fear of massive lay offs after privatization is a major deterrent to privatization.

Thus enterprise reform is the core problem in Eastern Europe. Moreover, as privatization ran into delays, a new problem emerged. It is probably possible to run a SOE efficiently, and it is certainly possible to get efficiency from a private enterprise. What turns out to be impossible is to get efficiency from an enterprise whose ownership status is in limbo. Two years after the crumbling of central authority that used to exercise both ownership and control, ownership of SOEs remains ineffective and control diffuse. Without sharply defined control rights, various groups (workers, managers, local authorities) could only demonstrate their clout by disrupting the enterprise. Moreover, with changes in ownership announced but not implemented, managers and workers have every incentive to decapitalise the enterprise. Thus, two years after hyperinflation wiped out all nominal debts, 2000 out of Poland's 8000 major enterprises yet to be privatized are once again unable to service their debts.

The resulting debt overhang prevents straight auctioning. Outsiders cannot know whether the firm's distress situation is due to inefficient management, due to very efficient management responding to perverse incentives or due to the fact that the firm has no prospects even under the best of management practices. Thus enterprise restructuring has become unavoidable.

Objectives of a Sound Restructuring Plan

The core objective is to restore efficient employment of industrial assets. Solving the debt overhang of enterprises is a prerequisite for the wider objective. However, that is *not enough*. The debt problems arose for a reason; if that root cause is not addressed, the problems will likely reoccur in a few years. Thus a restructuring plan needs to include safeguards against reoccurrence.

Experience in Eastern Europe indicates that clarification of medium term ownership structure should be the starting point of any plan. Similarly, clear assignment of control rights over the corporation is essential to stop the destructive fights over control and the decapitalization that are currently plaguing most enterprises. The first decision is whether the firm is to be privatized eventually or should remain in state hands. If state, the company should arguably be transferred to a separate agency. Incentive problems in permanent state enterprises are entirely different from those faced in enterprises about to be privatized; there is no obvious merit in combining their control in one agency.

For enterprises that will leave the state sector, re-establishing central control on an interim basis is unlikely to be effective. No governance scheme is effective if privatization will take place 'somewhere' in the future, since managers then always have incentives to decapitalise the firm and buy off worker unrest through excessive wage increases. Thus the best safeguard against reoccurrence of debt problems is a substantial acceleration of the privatization effort.

For firms that are still servicing their debts, privatization should work; a positive cash flow after debt service means that a positive price is feasible through auction or bilateral negotiation. This does not necessarily have to involve cash up front; a case can be made for non-cash offers, such as bank funded management buy outs. Otherwise wealth constraints might limit the set of potential bidders too much, leaving out potentially better entrepreneurs because of ineffective capital markets.

However, auctioning off enterprises with a heavy debt burden will most likely fail; under present management practice most of them are insolvent, which precludes straight auctioning off since auctions require a positive price. A negative price cash auction result would transfer two things to a 'buyer': a lump sum payment plus a negative net worth company (otherwise the cash payment would not be necessary to begin with). Clearly the optimal thing to do for the buyer is to simply take the money and walk away from the company, which presumably would once again mean state ownership. The net result would then be a cash transfer but no privatization. The problems with negative price cash auctions do not mean that heavily indebted firms should not be privatized, but that their debts need to be reduced prior to privatization.

Liquidation is likely to be unduly destructive; poor performance in many cases reflects as much distorted management incentives as real insolvency assuming sensible management incentives. A more efficient way of debt restructuring would use the opportunity to introduce effective ownership. This suggests that conversion of some of the debt into equity should be the focal point of the restructuring exercise. Debt equity conversion offers a more promising way towards efficient use of the assets controlled by the enterprises than liquidation into a thin capital market and a depressed economy.

Privatizing Profitable Industries

Privatization is clearly the answer to Eastern Europe's problems, and should be done fast. Nevertheless no country has been able to implement privatization at a significant scale beyond single-establishment service sector firms. So why is privatization so much more difficult than initially thought?

Three major issues stand out. The *first* issue derives from the most striking difference between SOEs in Eastern Europe and say Mexico and the UK: their state enterprises, by the time privatization came under consideration, were tightly controlled by an effective central authority. The situation was the same in Eastern Europe until recently;

but it was this very central authority that was completely discredited during the collapse of communism. Since then control of SOEs has been diffuse, with several groups vying for a dominant position: workers, incumbent managers, and local governments.[1] The battle for enterprise control has not only crippled the current operations of SOEs throughout Eastern Europe, but has also effectively precluded privatization. With nobody exercising effective control, nobody can transfer it either.

Some have therefore called for renationalization prior to privatization, but this is not a solution: if central authorities would be able to implement such a solution, they would not have lost control in the first place. The proper response probably requires buying off those groups powerful enough to block privatization, possibly by transfer of shares as part of the privatization. Such elements have been built in the process in Poland, but apparently not enough and not well enough targeted. There are political problems with this advice; the former power brokers (the 'Nomenklatura') are among those to be bought off. However the economic costs of locking them out might well be prohibitive, in the end leaving everybody worse off.

The *second* problem stems from the employment effects of privatization. So far privatization has led to layoffs of about 50% of the workers. This explains why workers have resisted privatization. Western style safety net institutions are not of much help: to leave workers near their previous level of income would lead to totally unaffordable schemes which moreover would destroy adjustment incentives. We return to this issue below.

The *third* problem is that the administrative requirements of the various schemes are beyond most East European governments' administrative capacity. There is really no solution other than slowing down and focusing foreign technical assistance on the privatization agency.

Enterprise Restructuring and Privatization

Straight privatization will not succeed for enterprises that do not generate enough cash flow to service their current debt and leave some income for residual claimants. Those firms may however be salvageable at lower levels of debt; they are thus candidates for restructuring. Six principles should underlie debt-restructuring.

Avoid large-scale liquidation. The idea that an entire industrial sector is unsalvageable makes little sense. A large part of GDP (a value added concept!) is produced in manufacturing; this means per definition that a capital structure and set of wage contracts can be designed under which most of the sector can operate profitably. Moreover, most of the problems stem from distorted incentive structures in the past rather than incompetent management; and even in the latter case the right solution would be to replace management, not necessarily to break up the firm. In most of Eastern Europe firms are excessively vertically integrated; this was the only way input supplies could be arranged under central planning. But this problem calls for splitting the firm into smaller firms during privatization, not for asset stripping.

Avoid bankruptcy procedures. Use of bankruptcy procedures would inevitably overload the system and lead to interminable legal delays, thus prolonging the limbo on ownership and effective control that is behind much of the SOE crisis to begin with. This requires more than just a decision not to use bankruptcy courts in the workout scheme. In particular, the next point needs to be resolved if excessive use of bankruptcy courts is to be avoided.

Resolve conflicts between creditors without triggering unnecessary liquidation. Any debt workout has to reconcile different creditor interest. If a senior creditor imposes a solution that another creditor considers unfair or less favourable than straight liquidation, that other creditor will derail the programme by triggering bankruptcy procedures. Thus the workout scheme needs to incorporate mechanisms for resolving creditor conflicts that will not trigger excessive liquidation proceedings.

Maintain incentives to not unload debt to the Government. Debt write-offs should be just enough to restore solvency, but not more than that. Excessive unloading of debt onto the Government adds to an already difficult macro-management problem: the tax system is strained to the limits to finance current expenditure plans in a non-inflationary manner. Thus debt restructuring should be costly to management and commercial banks.

Bias debt restructuring towards debt/equity conversion. This is a trend in bankruptcy reform since it allows the firm to continue as a going concern and avoids the firesale problems associated with liquidation. A creditor is always better off than if it writes the loans off; equity cannot fall below zero so is at worst equivalent to a write off, but if the firm's fortunes improve, the creditor will share in the upswing.

Commercial banks should play a substantial role. Converting bank debts into equity creates concentrated share ownership, so at least one group of shareholders has the ability and incentives to actively monitor managers. Ownership of equity by commercial banks does cause regulatory problems; it makes capital adequacy difficult to assess, since the shares are likely to remain non-traded in most cases. However, the regulatory problem is likely to be minor for some time if banks are recapitalized up front on the basis of a conservative assessment of the status of the loan that is to be converted into equity. And as time goes by and the regulatory problem grows, the banks can be made to sell off the equity gradually.

A Practical Proposal

Creditors can be subdivided into three classes: *one*, and most senior, the Government through tax arrears, social security claims and so on. *Two*, bank credit and secured non-bank creditors; *three*, interenterprise credits. At the bottom of all this is the ultimate owner, the Government. The proposal aims at privatization of the restructured enterprise, and relies heavily on the commercial banks to resolve the administrative capacity constraints on privatization agencies.

The approach takes its cue from a recent proposal for bankruptcy reform, modifying it so as to turn it into a method for privatization.[2] It consists of two parts, a way of soliciting reorganization proposals and a method of debt restructuring. The method of debt restructuring is best explained by example. Take the case of two creditors, say tax arrears and a commercial bank, of $100 and $200 respectively. The scheme implies four steps:

1. Write off all debts;
2. Creation of equity (in this case 100 shares of $1) *all of which goes to the senior creditor, here the Government.*
3. The junior creditor receives *a call option* on those shares with exercise price of $1 per share. The bank will exercise this option if the value of the firm without any debt exceeds the value of the Government's claims (which the Government could scale back).
4. Managers and workers receive call options with exercise price of $3, which means exercising them will allow all senior creditors to be paid off. Alternatively, such residual claims could be auctioned off.

Simultaneously, the administrator of the scheme solicits reorganization proposals from the creditors, from workers and/or incumbent management, or from outside investors. The shareholders emerging from this process vote on the proposals for reorganization or reject them all, in which case liquidation becomes unavoidable.

Viable reorganization proposals could come from foreigners or outside domestic investors, with cash injection; or from incumbent management without cash injection. The scheme allows for *non-cash-management-buy-outs*: commercial banks could, instead of exercising their own options, finance management's exercising the lower level options it receives under this scheme.

This plan solves a series of problems. First, seniority of claims is preserved, which facilitates reaching an agreement; no junior creditor will have an incentive to derail the procedure by triggering bankruptcy. Furthermore the scheme creates a class of equity holders seriously interested in proper management of the companies; and it accelerates privatization. Finally, the scheme allows non-cash management buy-outs. This is important; incumbent management is typically best informed about the firm's potential but may be wealth-constrained and so unable to compete in an all-cash auction.

Dealing with Large Enterprises

This approach might in the end still leave authorities with companies that nobody wants, with or without pre-existing debt. For relatively small firms, straight liquidation is possible. Realism and humanitarian concerns suggest that such drastic actions may not work for very large enterprises or dominant employers in poor regions. Here a more gradual approach seems unavoidable.

Keeping such loss makers temporarily afloat is a sort of *workfare*; since the alternative is unemployment, the government could consider keeping the workers productively engaged. As long as they produce enough value added to pay the excess of their own wages over what they would cost the government in unemployment pay, the Government gains from a fiscal point of view.

There is an argument against such schemes: by providing dead-end jobs only, workers are not re-integrated in the economy and may in fact be discouraged from trying to be, since their income hinges on *not* moving away from their current location.

Thus, shielding large enterprises or regionally dominant employers from closure may be efficient compared to alternatives, but only temporarily so. But commercial banks may be singularly ill-suited to implement gradual closure. If the enterprise is big enough to effectively blackmail the government into not closing it down now, there is no reason to expect that a commercial bank (or for that matter the government itself) will be any more successful later. Simply imposing cash constraints is unlikely to be a credible threat; once again, if the government can be blackmailed into putting up the cash now, why should the firm not succeed again once the first allotment runs out?

The special nature of the problem first of all suggests that management of these 'workfare firms' should be transferred to an agency that is keenly aware of budget constraints, such as the finance ministry; and second that a major effort should be made to retrain the work force and assist it in finding alternative employment and housing. Absent such an assistance programme, claims of support being only temporary are simply not credible and will almost certainly be broken.

Employment Consequences: Which Policies can Help?

Labour market problems are the most visible and politically most sensitive of all transition problems. They are particularly costly in Eastern Europe because of the absence of institutions to provide a fallback to those becoming unemployed; at the same time, the experience in Western Europe strongly suggests that simply providing such institutions could, while lowering the social costs of unemployment, also contribute to its almost indefinite extension. Western Europe is rich enough to afford such inefficient largesse, but the East clearly is not. The core problem is to provide such assistance without destroying adjustment incentives.

A starting point is the observation that one-off large sectoral shocks create different problems than the fluctuations associated with business cycles. Western safety nets are designed to provide income support during periods of temporary unemployment after which the worker is expected to be back to the same or a similar job. They do not deal at all with the special problems created by *permanent* sectoral and regional shocks, and accordingly have been singularly unsuccessful in dealing with them.

At the core of transitional problems are *informational problems* and *skill mismatches.* Workers losing their job in one industry might be willing to take up jobs in another, but do not know about them and cannot afford the job search. Clearly such problems are greatly exacerbated if there is a regional aspect to them. Regional unemployment not only raises the difficulty of obtaining adequate information about job opportunities, but also adds the often substantial costs of relocation and housing provision if a job match is found.

Even with adequate provision of information, problems may still arise because of skill mismatches. A lifelong experience in building tanks does not help when starting on the assembly of computer memories. What this really means is that human capital loses much of its value when patterns of labour demand shift. The social costs may be high and resistance to the subsequent decline in living standards may threaten the sustainability of the reforms.

So what can the Government do? We focus on three areas: training programmes, capital market intervention and public works. Successful adjustment programmes, like Japan's in the seventies, emphasized *training.* Setting up successful training programmes is fraught with problems however. The key question is: train people for what? Unless some private sector involvement can be solicited, placing trainees can be difficult.

Efforts to solve this problem through tax incentives have tended to produce only short term relief; often trainees are fired once the tax benefits end. Mexico tried an alternative approach: companies organize the training with government subsidies and technical assistance; in this set up, jobs are assured since the firm, which has to share in the costs by paying the worker a wage while on training, presumably would not make this investment unless it intends to reap the benefits in the future. Paying workers while on training also builds an element of income support into the programme.

Making firms share in the costs increases the chance that the training will be properly directed, but raises the informational problems mentioned before. After all, such cost sharing comes from new employers, not from the old, so the match between worker and firm still needs to be made. This is in particular a problem if regional location of old and new firms are different. This requires integration of data bases of regional employment offices, and national advertising of vacancies.

Japan follows a different approach to this issue. In large diversified industrial groups the match can be made internally, using the

companies' own training facilities. The Government itself has set up
hundreds of training centres for the use of smaller and less diversified
firms. Moreover, contrary to practice elsewhere, Japanese firms have to
pay a large share of the wages of laid off workers, and therefore have a
strong incentive to assist laid off workers in finding jobs elsewhere. It
is not uncommon for firms to actually contact target firms and make
arrangements for salary transfers on condition that the new firm takes
over some of the redundant workers.

Even if training facilities are provided, *capital market problems*
might prevent their effective use. Any move into new lines of work by
either firms or workers will initially involve negative cash flows. This
could be because of retraining expenses or job search by workers, need
for relocation, re-tooling or investment outlays by firms. Thus, access
to credit is particularly important. Unfortunately, reorientation means
both a decline in value of current assets and therefore diminished col-
lateralization possibilities, and at the same time higher uncertainty
about future earnings. Thus access to credit markets is likely to be
impaired at the very time it is most needed. For this reason successful
restructuring programmes often include a credit component conditional
on submittal of restructuring plans. This was the case in Australia after
agriculture support prices were phased out in the seventies and in the
Japanese 'Smaller Enterprise Business Switchover Act'.

Is there a role for more active public involvement via public investment? There is evidence of a complementarity between public investment in infrastructure and private investment. Roads towards a village
increase the chances that somebody will build a plant in that village.
Thus private investment response could well be stronger if public
investment in infrastructure is to some extent shielded from the budget
cutting that fiscal sustainability requires. Public sector investment projects geared towards private sector productivity improvement (by better roads, access to electricity, investment in training facilities etc.) can
play a useful role in industrial policy packages; during implementation
labour is absorbed, while a positive impact on private productivity
means that private demand for labour increases once the projects are
finished.

Key to Mexico's relative ease of adjustment has been an imaginative
public works programme administered through local authorities. This
programme, by design, allows fine regional targeting and has incentives built in towards reducing bureaucracy and increasing local participation. The program (PRONASOL, a Spanish acronym for programme

for national solidarity) consists of block grants from the centre to *municipal authorities.* They can use this money as they see fit under the following rules. *First,* it can only be spent on materials; labour has to be provided for free by the community. This makes sure that only projects the community actually wants are chosen; otherwise they would not donate their labour.[3] *Second,* projects have to be approved in open municipal meetings, to eliminate corruption and diversion of funds to local authorities' own pockets.

Introduction of programmes like this in Eastern Europe would introduce an employment support programme that does not involve open ended budget commitments, since it is block grant based; it would self-select only those out of work by offering below market wages; it would allow a cheap way of building up infrastructure and this is likely to encourage matching private investment; and finally it allows regional targeting, important given the regional structure of unemployment in most East European countries. A particularly useful focal point would be to finance housing construction through such a programme, since this would address one of the most serious barriers to mobility currently holding back labour market adjustment.

Conclusions

Our guiding theme has been that Eastern Europe is not well served with straight textbook advice. The common wisdom on privatization fails to address the problems created by the diffuse ownership and control prior to privatization. Cash auctions may not efficiently match managers and capital stock because of wealth constraints. Standard advice on enterprise restructuring fails to incorporate the consequences of the sheer scale of the problem, and of the reasons why current profits are a poor guide to future profit opportunity. Finally, introducing Western style unemployment insurance, while lowering the social costs of unemployment, would almost certainly contribute to its indefinite extension.

These problems can be addressed by incorporating incentive problems specific to Eastern Europe into policy design. Sometimes the resulting advice is novel and as yet untried; in some cases successful examples exist. Thus some experimentation is unavoidable. The alternative, however, is declining incomes and increasing social unrest as the consensus underlying the reforms erodes.

Reference

O. Blanchard, K. Froot, J. Sachs (eds), The Transition in Eastern Europe, NBER and Univesity of Chicago Press, forthcoming 1993.

Notes

1 A vivid account of this process in Russia is given by Schleifer and Vishny (1992), *Privatization in Russia*, in The Transition in Eastern Europe, NBER and University of Chicago Press, forthcoming 1993.
2 See Aghion, Hart and Moore (1992), *The Economics of Bankruptcy Reform*, in The Transition in Eastern Europe, NBER and University of Chicago Press, forthcoming 1993.
3 Wage payments below the going rate would still preserve this 'screening aspect' to some extent, while introducing an element of income support.

Economic Disintegration: Are There Cures?

SPECIAL MERIT AWARD

Summary

The (re)appearance of economic nationalism in the disintegration former Soviet and Yugoslav federations has significantly worsened their economic collapse. This essay examines the pathology of economic nationalism and proposes a remedy.

A look back to the dissolution of the Habsburg Empire illustrates the potential costs of intense nationalism swapping over into the economic sphere. Today bears a striking resemblance to the early 1920s. The dinar zone has fragmented, the ruble zone totters on the brink. Trade between the successor states has shrunk dramatically, with production following suit. The cause of the malaise is readily spotted. Uncertainty about the policies of other republics and a desire to obtain bargaining chips motivates rounds of retaliatory export restrictions. The resulting protectionism is self-sustaining: even though all republics may desire a *joint* return to free trade, no republic has an incentive to move first. The cure against economic nationalism must hence involve a credible coordination mechanism, including a stick as well as the carrot of better export markets.

This essay considers both a Russia-led and an IMF-led scheme, concluding in favour of the latter. The proposed scheme is based on two elements. First, an extension of IMF conditionality to explicitly incorporate a republic's acceptance of a minimal code of conduct regarding monetary and trade relations. Second, the creation of a temporary payments union as a second best measure to stabilize trade until monetary hardening and marketization have sufficiently progressed to allow the adoption of first best institutional arrangements.

Holger C. Wolf, a German national, is an Assistant Professor of Economics and International Business at the Stern School of Business, New York University. He has previously worked as a consultant on monetary reform to the Renaissance Foundation in Ukraine and on unification economics to the World Bank. He has published a number of articles on monetary history, postwar European reconstruction and the East European transition.

4

Economic Disintegration: Are There Cures?

HOLGER C. WOLF

At a time when Western Europe is moving towards closer monetary and economic ties, political emancipation in the former Yugoslav and Soviet Confederations has been accompanied by monetary beggar thy neighbour policies and growing protectionism. The high degree of economic interdependence between the successor states renders the emergent economic nationalism very costly: output declines in the two former federations have far exceeded those in the other transition economies. The economics and politics of disintegration largely remain uncharted territory. This essay comments on the pathology of economic nationalism before examining potential cures.

The analysis begins with a look back to the dissolution of the Austrian-Hungarian dual monarchy as another instance of mutually hostile independence movements successfully exploiting the collapse of central authority. Then, as now, appeals by the international community urging economic cooperation and integration[1] went unheeded as ethnic conflicts spilt over into the economic sphere: '*Political subjection had too long been identified in their minds with economic domination, and political nationalism found an equally distinct counterpart in economic nationalism*'.[2] The emergent economic nationalism proved costly: two of the three successor states suffered hyperinflation; trade and production suffered sizeable declines.

The same volatile mix of nationalism and economic crisis threatens another occurrence of the protectionist malady in the former Soviet Union (FSU) and Yugoslavia.[3] After a brief review of developments to date, a set of institutional reforms to mitigate the costs of economic nationalism is proposed.

1. Lessons From The Past

The study of the dissolution of the Habsburg Empire reveals striking parallels to today's developments: '*Coming into existence as a result of the violent disruption of old relationships, in a strained atmosphere of war and revolution, the new [. . .] countries could not escape extreme manifestations of political nationalism, which was intensified by the fact that large numbers [. . .] found themselves [. . .] in the condition of minorities in the newly created states. And side by side with this aspect of their new nationhood these countries were confronted with economic problems of great magnitude and complexity.*'[4]

The dual monarchy had balanced agricultural areas in Hungary with industrial areas in Austria, yielding overall near self-sufficiency: more than 70 percent of Hungary's exports were destined for Austria and vice versa. In principle, economic cooperation could have continued despite the political disintegration. In practice, new found sovereignty was held to require economic autonomy: '*Political independence appeared most precarious without economic independence.*'[5]

On the trade side, several rounds of retaliation translated minor impediments into prohibitive barriers; government barter replaced commercial trade. Having adopted positions of extreme protectionism—not least in order to obtain bargaining chips—the successor governments proceeded to negotiate reductions. The protectionist setting proved however to be quite resistant to reform efforts. While the successor governments concurred in lamenting the present state of affairs and agreed that, in principle, a liberalization would be mutually advantageous, no individual government proved willing to take the initiative in dismantling barriers.[6]

The ensuing trade and production contraction was worsened by continuing monetary instability. Following the suspension of reserve requirements in 1914, the Austrian-Hungarian Bank (AHB) had monetized the deficit throughout the war, resulting in a fourteenfold increase in money supply. Following the collapse, the successor states initially adopted the institutional remnants of the Austrian-Hungarian system, including the Crown as legal tender. The fragile union however did not last long. The sound money objectives espoused by Czechoslovakia clashed with the desire for further deficit monetization in Austria and Hungary. Failing in her attempts to either convince the Allies to assume control of the AHB or to negotiate a monetary rule of conduct

built around unanimity in emission decisions, Czechoslovakia seceded
from the Crown zone, enforcing monetary reforms by the other successor states.

Over the next four years, Austria and Hungary underwent
hyperinflation. Czechoslovakia, while avoiding extreme monetary
instability by dint of her fiscal and monetary conservatism, nevertheless suffered from the monetary disintegration, initially by a contagion
effect from the Mark and Austrian Crown, later, as the Crown turned
into the 'dollar of central Europe', by a sizeable real appreciation.

The experience of Austria-Hungary amply demonstrates that
although in principle economic cooperation need not suffer from
changing frontiers, the political attraction of economic nationalism can
easily lead to a negative sum game with escalating trade conflicts and
monetary beggar thy neighbour policies. The sensitivity of sound economics to the politics of the day was as apparent then as it is today:
'*the atmosphere of mutual distrust and of political fears played an
exceedingly important role*'.[7] Once reached, the protectionist outcome
becomes hard to dislodge without a formal coordination and enforcement mechanism. The ensuing avoidable collapse in trade and production motivates a search for institutional structures better equipped to
avoid a repeat of the mistakes of the 1920s in the coming years.

2. Economic Disintegration Today

The current upheaval in the Soviet and Yugoslav federations is reminiscent of the dissolution of the Habsburg Empire. Again long sup-
pressed ethnic conflicts are flaring up; political nationalism threatens to
swap over into the economic sphere.

The breakdown of central authority has severed the established supply links. Receiving increasingly fewer supplies from the centre and
lacking a readily available alternative exchange mechanism, republican
governments react with export restrictions on foodstuffs, raw materials
and subsidized products. The resources thus obtained are subsequently
used as bargaining chips in inter-governmental barter deals which
increasingly attempt to offset deliveries and counterdeliveries so as to
achieve bilateral trade balance with little if any monetary settlements.

The ruble zone meanwhile totters on the brink of dissolution.
Russia's unilateral decision to (re)nationalize the ruble deprived the
other republics of seigniorage, monetary control and not least cash,

prompting both the issue of temporary coupons as complementary monies and announcement of future secession from the ruble zone. The proliferation of emission centres and quasi monies complicates monetary control and increases uncertainty, further undermining monetary trade. Monetary growth shows clear signs of acceleration. Note emission is set to double between January and July; credit expansion proceeds virtually unchecked; inter-enterprise debt has multiplied twentyfold from January to May.

The outlook is grim: the restrictive forces exerted by the lacking financial sophistication of the successor states and the—already leaking—insulation between credit and cash will not be effective much longer. At this state, a deterioration of inflation—already at 700 percent—into hyperinflation appears more likely than a rapid return to monetary stability.

The costs of economic nationalism are clearly discernible. Increasing uncertainty about the future legal and economic status of the ruble renders monetary trade unattractive, forcing republics into bilaterally balanced barter deals. The extreme degree of inter-republican dependence (Tables 1 and 2) translates attempts at bilateral balance into a severe trade contraction. Despite the partial price reform, the efficiency of the current trade pattern falls far short of the previous system built around a single central authority.

Table 1 Regional Dependence: Yugoslavia

	Relative GSP per capita	Production Share Going To		
		Home Market	Other Regions	Exports
Slovenia	198	58	20	22
Croatia	127	67	19	10
Vojvodina	118	58	29	10
Serbia	103	62	17	10
Montenegro	73	58	25	11
Bosnia-Herzegovina	68	56	24	14
Macedonia	66	61	21	9
Kosovo	25	65	24	9

Source: Statistical Yearbooks, IMF.

Table 2 Regional Dependence: FSU

	Relative GSP per capita	Total Trade (% of GNP)	FSU Trade (% of Total)
Belarus	119	52.0	85.8
Russia	119	22.3	57.8
Latvia	106	54.1	86.7
Lithuania	101	54.5	86.8
Estonia	93	58.9	85.1
Georgia	93	43.8	86.5
Ukraine	90	34.0	79.1
Armenia	88	53.7	89.2
Moldova	87	52.2	87.9
Kazakhstan	72	34.2	86.3
Azerbaijan	71	41.3	85.7
Kirgizia	57	45.6	87.1
Turkmenistan	53	42.2	89.1
Uzbekistan	47	39.7	85.9
Tajikistan	44	43.7	86.3

Sources: Pisani-Ferry and Sapir (1992), IMF, Deutsche Bank (1991).

3. Looking Forward: Options

Trade and production in the FSU and Yugoslavia have collapsed. Part of the decline reflects the unavoidable costs of transition, yet a significant fraction must be attributed to the—avoidable—resurgence of economic nationalism. As in the 1920s the successor states agree—in principle—that a reduction in trade barriers and monetary hardening would be desirable. Indeed, the communiques of the Brussels conferences are strikingly reminiscent of their antecedents in the Portrose conference of 1922. Yet, now as then, progress towards implementation proceeds at a snail's pace, raising the spectre of a repeat appearance of the interwar dilemma: agreement in principle and inaction in particulars.

The cause of the malaise is readily spotted. Uncertainty about the policies of other republics coupled with a desire to obtain bargaining chips for future negotiations renders the retention of scarce goods within a republic's boundary the obvious immediate choice. In contrast to free trade, the resulting protectionism is self-sustaining: even though all republics may (indeed, do) agree that a *joint* return to free trade would be mutually beneficial, no republic has an incentive to move first. In like vein, monetary beggar thy neighbour policies remain individually attractive even though a joint return to sound money would be mutually beneficial.

The cure against economic nationalism must therefore be built around a credible coordination mechanism, including a stick as well as the carrot of greater access to export markets and monetary stability.[8] This essay examines two options, relying respectively on Russia and the IMF to take on the coordination role. Following this analysis, specific arrangements to mitigate the potential costs of economic nationalism are discussed.

3.1 Internal Coordination: Russia

As yet, the West has not taken a leading role in coordinating trade and monetary reform, tacitly relying on Russia to prod the other republics along. The Russian leadership approach relies on exploiting the asymmetry of bargaining power within the FSU: reflecting her size and her control over a large share of energy resources, Russia stands to suffer *relatively* little from any bilateral trade conflict and may hence be able to credibly threaten sanctions against non-conforming republics.

Table 3 illustrates the distribution of relative bargaining power. The first column reports the loss (as a fraction of total output) a republic would incur if trade in 'soft' goods without alternative markets outside the FSU were to stop. With the exception of Russia and Kazakhstan, republics stand to lose between a quarter and half of their production, underlining the prime importance of intra-republican trade. Column two reports the loss to Russia if trade with the particular republic would stop, and column 3 reports the *ratio* of losses to the republic and to Russia. With the exception of Ukraine, losses to Russia from particular bilateral trade disturbances are fairly minor and, with the exception of Kazakhstan, the loss to the republic would exceed the loss to Russia herself.

An internal coordination with Russia assuming the leadership role—the current setting—thus appears principally feasible. However, several problems arise. First, reliance on internal coordination assumes that progress towards marketization in Russia itself is irreversible,

Table 3 Relative Bargaining Power

	Loss From Disruption of Trade Percent of Net Material Product		
	Republic	Russia	Ratio
Russia	11.5	...	...
Kazakhstan	12.5	1.3	0.7
Ukraine	24.2	4.8	1.3
Uzbekistan	26.6	1.0	1.5
Turkmenistan	28.2	0.2	1.6
Tajikistan	31.7	0.2	1.8
Georgia	35.9	0.5	2.0
Azerbaijan	36.4	0.5	2.0
Kirgizia	38.3	0.2	2.1
Moldova	45.0	0.4	2.5
Lithuania	46.2	0.4	2.6
Armenia	50.3	0.3	2.8
Estonia	51.1	0.2	2.8
Latvia	52.1	0.3	2.9
Belarus	52.9	1.2	2.9

Source: Nuti and Pisani-Ferry (1992).

which appears by no means assured. Second, the internal coordination model runs into potential problems if the narrow interests of Russia diverge from the interests of the FSU in its entirety. Third, a Russia (Moscow) led reform will, rationally or not, encounter substantial political resistance from republican governments deriving a large part of their legitimization from opposition against the pervasive influence of Moscow.

3.2 External Coordination: IMF

These caveats suggest that reliance on internal coordination may yet again fail, as it did in the 1920s. Then, the appointment of League of Nations' commissioners with effective veto power for fiscal and monetary decisions proved instrumental in returning Austria and Hungary to sound policies. Today, foreign economic dictators—of the benevolent kind—are not (yet?) in the political picture. Nevertheless, the West can play an important role in ensuring a safe entry of the new republics into the group of democratic market economies. The IMF, combining a pool of technical knowledge with neutrality regarding inter-republican conflicts and a strong bargaining chip in its ability to affect access to international capital markets provides the natural candidate for the external coordinator.

4. A Reform Package

How is the IMF to perform its role? The policy challenge is twofold. The creation of sound convertible currencies will even under optimistic assumptions take another year or two. Continuation of the collapse in trade and production until then risks undermining the political support for reforms. A resuscitation of at least a modicum of trade even in the absence of a healthy monetary system thus assumes prime importance. The objective can be achieved via a temporary payments union, the first pillar of the proposed reform package. In the medium run, a return to sound money and a substantial softening of trade barriers are prerequisites for a successful transition. The adoption of a minimal code of conduct regarding trade and monetary interaction within the FSU provides the second pillar of the reform package. The IMF—appropriately seconded by her sister organization, the World Bank—can play a crucial role in coordinating both stages, first by encouraging the adoption of a payments union and second by extending conditionality to include acceptance of the code of conduct.

   Reform in the FSU thus requires a careful balance between macroeconomic *re*-centralization and microeconomic *de*-centralization. While the contraction in trade and production motivates attempts to preserve temporarily part of the existing trade and monetary links, long term success of the reforms requires many of these links to disappear as enterprises adjust to the new environment with radically different relative prices, higher transportation and energy costs and increased access to other trading partners. The objective for institutional reform is to devise structures that safeguard against excessive short term contraction while permitting long term adjustment.

4.1 The Payments Union

The monetary situation in the FSU is rapidly deteriorating. Uncertainty about the future has all but eliminated ruble based trade. Settlement in hard currencies provides no alternative as republics attempt to preserve scarce reserves for purchases of hard goods. The result is a regression to bilaterally balanced barter, resulting in a severe trade contraction. In the medium run, stabilization will do much to revive monetary trade. However, a return to monetary stability cannot be expected for at least a year. A continued trade and production collapse imposes severe political cost, motivating the search for a temporary arrangement enabling a limited revival of multilateral trade even in the absence of a sound monetary system. The proposal for a payments union aims to fulfil that role.[9]

The payments union improves on the current situation in two ways. First, it enables a return to multilateralism by permitting offsets of bilateral surpluses and deficits and provides for some short run flexibility by providing prespecified credit quotas. In addition to permitting short run trade stabilization, the union provides a natural coordination mechanism for reducing trade barriers and (by means of a gradual reduction of the credit quotas beyond which settlement in hard currency is required) of convergence towards full convertibility. The EPU of postwar western Europe provides a useful role model in both respects.

The role of the West in regard to the payments union is threefold. First, to provide the start up funding. The positive effect of a union on trade and hence production suggests that these resources—in any case refundable—would probably reduce the total outlay otherwise necessary to stabilize the FSU. Secondly, to provide the technical expertise, drawn from the experiences of the EPU and thirdly, to run the system as a neutral agent.

4.2 A Code of Conduct

The payments union, by allowing a return to multilateralism irrespective of the monetary instability and the level of trade restrictions, acts as a short run tranquillizer while not addressing the underlying causes.[10] The dissimilarity between the republics in combination with the politics of secession suggests that highly integrated reforms—the creation of a customs union or a convertible ruble zone—are unlikely. In the medium run, substantial variability in trade regimes and monetary stringency can be expected. The second pillar of the proposed reform package has the twofold aim of eliminating the most harmful variants of monetary and trade policies while creating a policy structure that, while flexible, allows a gradual convergence towards more uniform policies in the future.

4.2.1 Trade

The desirable long term trading system combines full convertibility with low internal and external tariff barriers. In the short run, the emergence of any structure even approaching a free trade zone remains highly unlikely as the market infrastructure does not yet exist and as republic governments are as yet unwilling to surrender control over 'crucial' sectors. The short run equilibrium will thus unavoidably involve considerable managed trade. The challenge is to construct rules that avoid trade collapse while encouraging a speedy transition from inter-republic barter to full current account convertibility. The first problem is addressed by the payments union. The adoption of a code of conduct regarding trade addresses the second.

The code of conduct is built around the core principles of unimpeded trade and non-discrimination. Going beyond these principles, the code has to specify (1) the conditions under which restrictions can be introduced, (2) the permissible instruments, (3) the rules governing the application of these instruments and (4) the mechanisms for resolving disputes. Finally, the code should be seen as a first step towards compliance with the GATT and hence permit a gradual convergence. In line with these principles, the proposed code of conduct encompasses these minimal provisions:[11]

1. *Non-intervention Default*—Individuals and enterprises are allowed to freely trade in goods and services unless specifically prohibited from so doing.

2. *Symmetry*—Trade regulations apply equally to all republics.

3. *Unrestricted Passage*—Goods in transit are not subjected to unwarranted delay. Transport fees do not exceed reasonable costs.

4. *Import Restrictions*—Tariffs take preference over quotas. If imposed, quota allocations are sold by unrestricted auction.

5. *Export Restrictions*—Export restrictions may only be imposed on products with regulated prices. Price report is to be urgently implemented.

6. *Uniformity*—Goods are grouped into at most three groups for tariff purposes.

7. *Disputes*—Disputes will be decided by an arbitration council. The decision is binding.

4.2.2 Money

A return to market based trade requires sound monies. The present institutional setup encouraged instead a fiscal deficit race as part of the inflation tax falls on the other republics. A monetary code of conduct aimed to restore at least a modicum of monetary stability hence forms the second pillar of the medium term reforms. Efforts at monetary stablization are of course contingent on the future monetary system. Three main variants can be distinguished. First, a continuation of the ruble zone. Second, a system of republican monies linked by fixed exchange rates. Third, a system of independent currencies. The third outcome seems most likely.

A continuation of the ruble zone is unlikely on both economic and political grounds. Economically, the current ruble zone does not constitute an optimal currency area. Politically, the symbolic quality of a separate money as an outward sign of political independence should not be underestimated. A system of irrevocably linked national currencies (based e.g. on currency boards) likewise appears unrealistic at this stage. Even if the necessary real exchange rate adjustments could be brought about solely through the wage mechanism, the differences between republics in terms of financial sophistication and fiscal yields and not least the potential of military conflict renders a replication of the Habsburg scenario more probable, with some republics reaching the shore of monetary stability fast while others succumb to an intermediate period of hyperinflation.

In this environment, the objective of a monetary code of conduct is to allow a civilized divorce of those republics opting for a separate currency while specifying a less inflationary temporary modus operandi for the rump ruble zone.[12] At present Russia monopolizes the printing presses and therewith the seigniorage revenues. The other republics, deprived of cash, respond with coupon issues and credit expansion, undermining Russia's monetary control. A return to a semblance of monetary order can be built around a compromise solution. In return for a prespecified share—based on relative GDP—of new ruble emissions and a say in the transitional management of the ruble zone, republics would undertake to retire ruble balances obtaining in any future secession from the ruble zone, as well as commit to an immediate cessation of coupon issues and a limit on credit expansion. The sharing rule must of course be augmented by limits on the total new emissions, specified as part of the ongoing IMF negotiations.

5. Conclusion

The political dissolution of the former Soviet and Yugoslav Federations has been accompanied by severe trade and output contractions. Part of the decline reflects the unavoidable costs of reconstructing a market economy. Yet resurgent economic nationalism significantly—and unnecessarily—worsens the contraction.

Economic recovery in the FSU ultimately depends on individuals grasping the chances offered by the market environment. Their ability to assume the initiative crucially depends on the return to sound monetary policies and a reduction of the protectionist mood. It is here that the West—wishing to safeguard the transition to democratic market economies—has a crucial role to play.

The problem, now as in the 1920s, is not that better policies are not known. Rather, the issue is missing coordination: a joint return to free(r) trade and monetary stability would be mutually beneficial, yet, stuck in a beggar thy neighbour world, it does not pay the individual republic to become charitable first. While the political will for continued reform has to come from within, the West can play a significant role in coordinating a return to sound money and liberalized trade. This paper concludes that the preferable strategy would be to render continued financial assistance conditional on the adoption of a minimal code of conduct for inter-republican monetary and trade relations. This conditionality needs to be strictly applied: the close linkages between the republics implies that failings in one republic reduce the recovery potential of the others. To stabilize trade in the short run, the code of conduct should be augmented by a self-liquidating payments union.

Commenting on the consequences of economic nationalism in the Habsburg successor states, Keynes argued that a Danubian Economic

Region 'might do as much for the peace and prosperity of the world as the League of Nations itself'. His assessment carries over to the new successor states.

References

Aghion, P., J. Flemming and J. Pisani-Ferry (1991); *A Framework For A Multilateral Clearing Scheme*; Mimeo, EBRD.

Asilis, Carlos and Stuart Brown (1991); *Western Aid And Soviet Reform: The Role of Coordination*; Georgetown University.

Berger, Peter-Robert (1982); Der Donauraum im wirtschaftlichen Umbruch nach dem Ersten Weltkreig; VWGO, Vienna.

Bofinger, P. (1991); 'Options for the Payments and Exchange Rate System in Eastern Europe'; *European Economy*, No. 2, 243–263.

Bofinger, P. (1992); 'Options for a New Monetary Framework For The Area of The Soviet Union'; *European Economy* 49.

Deutsche Bank (1991); *Die Sovietunion Im Umbruch*; Frankfurt.

Gros, Daniel, Jean Pisani-Ferry and André Sapir (1992) (eds.); *Inter-State Economic Relations In The Former Soviet Union*; CEPS Working Document No. 63.

Nuti, Mario and Jean Pisani-Ferry (1992); 'Post-Soviet Issues: Stabilization, Trade and Money', Mimeo.

Pasvolsky, Leo (1928): Economic nationalism of the Danubian States; Macmillan.

Pisani-Ferry, Jean and André Sapir (1992); *Trade and Transition to the Market: A Survey of the Key Issues*; in Daniel Gros et al. (eds.).

Williamson, J. (1992); *Soviet Monetary Disintegration Versus European Monetary Integration: Is Someone Making A Mistake?* Mimeo.

Notes

1 'The states which have been created . . . should at once re-establish full and friendly cooperation . . . in order that the essential unity of European economic life may not be impaired by the erection of artificial economic barriers', Allied Supreme Council Declaration March 8th, 1920.
2 Pasvolsky (1928).
3 For space reasons this essay will focus predominantly on the FSU.
4 Ibid.
5 Ibid.
6 Cf. Berger (1982).

7　Pasvolsky (1928).

8　Cf. Asilis and Brown (1991).

9　Cf. e.g. Aghion et al. (1991) and Bofinger (1991) *inter alia*.

10　Our focus is restricted to the structure of inter-republican relationships. Successful reform of course requires a host of other steps, most importantly price liberalization and a drastic increase in the lending rate.

11　See also Gros et al. (1992).

12　We are not concerned here with the optimal timing of monetary reform nor with the appropriate specification of the new monetary systems. For discussions of these issues see Bofinger (1992) and Williamson (1992), *inter alia*.

Regulatory Foundations for Global Capital Markets

SECOND PRIZE

Summary

The globalization of international capital markets has prompted widespread calls for international regulatory harmonization as an essential means of maintaining effective market regulation. This paper refutes the view that regulatory collusion is always preferable to regulatory competition, and lays a conceptual foundation for determining which regulatory issues should and should not be placed on the harmonization agenda.

Three distinct fundamental areas of capital market operation requiring regulatory attention are identified. Regulation may serve to reduce *systemic risk*, enhance *market efficiency* and promote equity, or *fairness*, in market operation. The position developed is that fairness as a regulatory objective should remain a matter of purely national concern, and that internationally-harmonized regulatory intervention is in principle only appropriate in addressing problems relating to systemic risk and market efficiency. Deriving the appropriate form of such intervention, however, requires a greater appreciation than has hitherto been shown for the multiple sources of risk and dimensions of efficiency.

Benn Steil is a Research Fellow in the International Economics Programme of the Royal Institute of International Affairs in London. Previously he held a Lloyd's of London Tercentenary Research Fellowship at Nuffield College, Oxford. His published research to date has been in the areas of currency risk management and behavioural and normative decision theory. He holds a BSc in Economics (1985) from the Wharton School of the University of Pennsylvania, and an MPhil in Management Studies (1988) and DPhil in Economics (1992) from Oxford University. In addition to his academic pursuits, Dr. Steil has worked in a permanent staff and consulting capacity for investment banks in New York and London, both in systems analysis and foreign exchange.

5

Regulatory Foundations for Global Capital Markets

BENN STEIL*

The past decade witnessed enormous changes in the structure and operation of international capital markets. Tremendous advances in information technology, increasing securitization of assets, the successful launch of new markets in derivative products, deregulation of financial markets, and the elimination of barriers to international capital flows have all contributed to a process of globalization in our capital markets. This process is now fuelling an ever-widening debate over how such markets can continue to be effectively regulated. This paper represents an attempt to define the conceptual foundations for a regulatory response to capital market globalization, and to highlight dimensions of the problem which are not presently being given sufficient consideration.

Regulatory Boundaries

The reality of a world divided into sovereign nation states means that the legal boundaries of a regulatory regime's jurisdiction are unlikely to correspond with those which pure economic efficiency considerations would define. The rapidly increasing integration among national economies means, however, that national sovereignty is becoming increasingly ineffectual as a source of both macro- and micro-economic control, and this trend must be acknowledged by policymakers if markets are to be effectively regulated. In an economic environment defined by high factor mobility, market forces will impose severe limitations on the ability of national authorities to control economic

* The author is grateful to Dirk Schoenmaker and Charles Goodhart for helpful comments on an earlier draft of this paper.

activities occurring within their borders without encouraging the migration of such activities to alternative jurisdictions.

Capital markets exist to redress the fundamental imbalance between sources of investable capital and locations of investment opportunities. As barriers to the flow of capital across national borders are steadily eliminated, financial markets become increasingly oblivious to the existence of such borders. While the effective regulation of our ever-expanding capital markets is growing in importance, the exceptionally high mobility of production factors in the financial services industry means that national authorities are losing their ability to dictate the form and extent of regulation. This development has led many to conclude that national authorities must arrive at binding agreements on harmonized regulations, and the more visionary to propose the creation of supranational regulatory authorities. Reasoning from integrated markets to legally integrated regulation is, however, an economic *non sequitur*.

Competition Among Rules

National economies remain embedded in distinct socio-legal frameworks, and this simple reality indicates both that *ex ante* harmonization will be difficult to implement and enforce and that significant scope remains for effective national regulation. Economic integration means, however, that national regulations must themselves be subject to foreign regulatory competition, and that ultimately the form and level of regulation will largely be determined by the jurisdictional arbitrage activities of those who are being regulated.

Those who would harmonize regulation by mandate often argue that the operation of competitive forces in a market for regulation must ultimately result in the elimination of regulation, which is presumed to be the preference of the regulated. As some basic level of public confidence in the stability and integrity of our capital markets must be maintained to keep them in operation, zero regulation is simply not a realistic possibility. It is, however, undoubtedly the case that the unfettered operation of regulatory arbitrage will not produce the same regulatory mix as a central authority with a captive regulatory clientele. The question should thus be whether competition among rules or collusion among rulemakers leads to more stable and efficient markets.

Regulatory Dialectics

Regulation is not a static control mechanism, but a dynamic interactive process. Regulators seek to control market activities in accordance with some regulatory objective function, but if these activities are profitable they will tend to migrate to alternative jurisdictions, re-label themselves, or mutate into regulation-resistant strains. Such manoeuvres provoke re-regulation by authorities in order to stem evasive practices, or induce attempts to create inter-jurisdictional regulatory cartels to stop 'cheating' amongst themselves; i.e. undercutting through unilateral cuts in a jurisdiction's regulatory 'price', or cost of operation. This in turn inspires another round of regulatory avoidance and re-regulation, as the dialectical process of political intervention and economic reorganization continues to unfold. This process has been well documented in explaining the historical development of the complex and inefficient structure of the US banking regulation bureaucracy.[1]

As capital markets evolve from national into global markets, the forces of regulatory arbitrage will become largely determinant in shaping the form and extent of market regulation in the absence of imposed international uniformity. The remainder of this essay attempts to lay the conceptual foundation for determining where such uniformity should be pursued, and where the forces of market and regulatory competition should be allowed to operate unfettered.

The *Raison d'Etre* of Regulation

The belief that global markets require global regulation has led to a research agenda focused on how to adapt all areas of regulation to the new economic environment. Unfortunately, sight has been lost of why it is we want to regulate capital markets in the first place, and it is only with reference to the explicit objectives of a given regulation that we can sensibly decide whether it must conform to some international standard or whether its ultimate specifications are best shaped through the competitive forces of international regulatory arbitrage.

A careful examination of capital market operations would indicate three distinct fundamental areas which require regulatory attention: these are *systemic risk*, *market efficiency*, and *fairness*. It is incumbent on policymakers to understand which of these areas a given regulation is designed to address. Without such an understanding, we run the serious risk of burdening our numerous international economic fora with a harmonization agenda that is both politically unmanageable and economically counterproductive.

1. Systemic Risk

Systemic risk is the market version of acid rain: it may be produced in only one jurisdiction, but its effects know no boundaries. The classic example in retail financial markets is the bank run, where fear of one bank failing leads to a mass withdrawal of funds from many banks, causing a collapse of the entire system. As any explicit or implicit government insurance guarantees represent a very real cost to taxpayers, while at the same time distorting the investment incentives of the beneficiaries, regulation must be designed to *reduce* rather than *eliminate* systemic risk.

The global integration process in capital markets means that the system with which policymakers are concerned extends over a multitude of regulatory jurisdictions. Since any systemic effects of inadequate or misguided regulation in one jurisdiction cannot be contained within that single jurisdiction, the imposition of universal standards or modes of operation is likely to be the only effective response.

The most fundamental barrier we face at present to defining such a response is an insufficient understanding of the *sources* of systemic risk in capital markets. Enormous political capital has already been sunk in establishing universal capital adequacy requirements, which reflect an underlying belief that *credit* or *position risk*[2] is the root threat to system stability. However, any market dive or crash will immediately re-ignite the debate over the effectiveness of the international settlements system; a concern which implies that systemic risk actually derives from *counterparty* risk.

Credit Risk

The 1988 Basle Accord established a minimum capital-asset ratio for all banks in the G-10 countries. A large number of assumptions lie behind the perceived need for a capital adequacy standard, but the most fundamental are that banks have been increasing their gearing towards dangerous levels, and that bank failures may result which could seriously threaten the stability of the entire financial system. Essentially, it is the risk of an institution's assets, relative to its capital base, which is presumed to underlie systemic risk.

With the road to Basle now widely seen as a sort of grand saga of Anglo-American political pluck and diplomatic ingenuity,[3] it is unlikely that the Accord's significant theoretical deficiencies and disregard for the mounds and trenches which still pock the 'levelled playing field' could actually provoke any significant reform.

Mutual distrust between politicians and economists notwithstanding, it is difficult to understand why regulators settled on a measure of bank asset portfolio risk which eschews the contributions of portfolio theory. The capital standards rely on a linear aggregation of risk-weighted asset values, where the risk weights are determined by regulatory fiat, and where covariances between asset values are ignored. Supporters of the Accord apparently like the relative 'simplicity' of the linear risk-weight method, and many believe it to be inherently more 'conservative'. Applying portfolio theory, however, requires nothing more than a spreadsheet, and contains no systematic bias toward lower capital requirements.[4]

As for the claim that universal capital standards level the international playing field, optimal capital structures, accounting for the social costs of systemic risk, cannot, even in principle, be determined without regard for tax structure or the level of implicit and explicit government insurance guarantees. Behind the myth of the level playing field also lies the blindest of faith that the law is impermeable and will effectively implement itself. In fact, loopholes in the Accord are numerous, and US banks have wasted no time in exploiting them.[5] There are also massive differences in the operation of regulatory systems in the G-10 countries, and we can fully expect national authorities to interpret the standards largely according to the dictates of their domestic regulatory clientele.

Reality will not stand in the way of progress, however, and discussions are well under way to extend capital adequacy requirements to securities firms. These requirements, we are assured, will be calculated so as to be consistent with achieving a level playing field for *all* financial services firms. Here it is clear that regulators have lost touch with their original objectives. Capital requirements were presumed needed to reduce systemic risk, and systemic risk was presumed to be institutionally dependent. But unless systemic costs are identical for banks and securities firms, and there is no reason to presume that they would be, then capital regulation must be institutionally based and hence incompatible with the objective of a level playing field.[6]

If credit or position risk is truly a significant contributor to systemic risk, we need a much clearer understanding of what factors motivate 'excessive' risk taking, and what coordinated measures can reasonably be expected to mitigate them.

Counterparty Risk

The arrangements under which trades are settled are a potentially significant source of systemic risk. The failure of a counterparty to fulfil its delivery or payment obligations can cause liquidity problems or solvency crises to ripple through the entire settlements system. Since there are dozens of different settlement systems operating in different markets and in very different legal environments, addressing the systemic implications of counterparty risk is a formidable challenge for regulators, but one for which a strong *prima facie* case can be made for some form of top-down harmonization.

Reducing the systemic risks deriving from counterparty risk involves two fundamental tasks. The first is to reduce the number of obligations which remain outstanding at any given time, and the second is to reduce the amount of time during which traders and clearing members are exposed to risk of counterparty failure. Both of these tasks rely on the efficient operation of a central clearinghouse.

Reducing the number of transactions is most effectively achieved through what is termed 'netting by novation'. When structured multilaterally, this system serves to reduce the interdependence of a network's members by netting out all their various obligations, creating one obligation from what may originally have been several. Such a system should also serve to reduce transaction costs.

The most significant barrier to the effective implementation of netting schemes is a legal one: the obligational restructuring which occurs under private netting arrangements is generally not legally recognized under insolvency law.[7] What is therefore required is a coordinated international effort to establish firm legal foundations for such systems. Once this is in place, the market may determine on its own the most efficient basis for netting obligations.

Reducing the time duration of counterparty risk is facilitated through the legal transference of all counterparty obligations in a given clearing system to its centralized clearinghouse. Concentrating default risk in a single institution, assuming that the risks are largely independent, allows for the efficient operation of portfolio effects. It also means that the stability of the entire network depends heavily on the financial integrity of this institution—and the bigger the institution the greater will be the financial shockwaves created by its fall.

Evaluating the Present Regulatory Agenda

The issues of clearing *efficiency* and clearinghouse *integrity* are high on the international regulatory agenda. Regulators should be sufficiently humble to recognize their limited abilities to improve the former, while explicitly acknowledging that they *already* bear significant responsibility for the latter.

There is a strong sense that some form of 'WorldClear'[8] system must ultimately be the most efficient response to capital market globalization. While there would appear to be significant economies of scale to be exploited in clearing activities, regulatory intervention to facilitate or mandate clearinghouse consolidation is inappropriate in the absence of strong evidence of cartel-like behaviour impeding it. Regulators are not in a position to make an *ex ante* determination of efficient institutional structures for clearing.

Regarding the financial integrity of clearinghouses, central banks already provide a variety of explicit and implicit payment guarantees which financially underpin clearing networks.[9] To the extent that such activities reduce systemic risk they may very well be desirable, but we cannot determine at present whether the regulatory benefits actually exceed the costs. This is because the taxpayers who are presently underwriting Central Bank insurance policies have never been sent the bill—no one has even attempted to calculate it.

What is needed is a coordinated international effort to determine what public guarantees are necessary and sufficient, who should provide them, and how their value can be effectively estimated and the cost allocated among the beneficiaries. It is too easy and tempting for regulators to cover up the potential costs of public guarantees when the risk of major failure *on their watch* is considered sufficiently small.

Systemic Risk and Regulatory Harmonization

The existence of significant systemic risk in international markets makes a strong *prima facie* case for regulatory harmonization from above. That it may be difficult to arrive at an appropriate basis for harmonization simply underscores the need for policymakers to be clear about the relationship between regulatory ends and means, and the importance of having the institutional capacity to implement and enforce regulations uniformly across jurisdictions.

2. Market Efficiency

Market participants will often require the intervention of an outside authority in order to ensure that contracts can be safely made and reliably enforced. Certification, disclosure requirements, and contract standardization are all forms of regulatory intervention which may serve to influence capital market structure and public confidence in a manner which enhances market efficiency. If markets which were previously national are now global, efficiency concerns should also provide *prima facie* support for top-down harmonization.

It is the rapid advancements in information technology made in recent years which is at the root of regulators' present concerns with market efficiency. Automated trading systems have proliferated, challenging the dominant positions of the traditional national and regional exchanges. This process has fuelled a growing debate over whether regulators should support one particular market structure over another (dealer market, open auction, or 'clearing-house' system), and whether market 'fragmentation' should be legally checked. The belief that international regulatory intervention is needed to ensure that markets remain integrated and efficient is, however, based on incomplete conceptions of *integration* and *efficiency*.

Market Integration

Trading at the best possible price at any given point in time requires a high degree of market *integration*, but not necessarily physical *consolidation*.[10] That is, buy and sell orders need not be channelled to a single trading location to ensure an efficient market price so long as effective arbitrage among the various marketplaces is possible. Ensuring effective integration may require regulators to mandate the provision of adequate intramarket linkages by all the constituent marketplaces, but it does not require constraints on what is effectively market *segmentation*. Competition among markets and trading systems is likely to act as a spur to innovation and efficiency, and should not be restrained on the basis of narrow conceptions of an 'integrated' market.

Market Efficiency: Whose Definition?

Allocative Efficiency

In evaluating market performance, economists generally focus on measures of *allocative efficiency*. Because a unitary measure of allocative efficiency in financial markets does not exist, it is extraordinarily difficult to estimate the net efficiency gains from even the most soundly formulated regulatory interventions.

In financial markets, allocative efficiency may be said to encompass two distinct measures of efficiency: *operational efficiency* and *pricing efficiency*.[11] Regulations aimed at increasing price transparency may increase the *operational efficiency* of the market by reducing the rents extracted by market intermediaries, but will damage *pricing efficiency* by driving intermediaries possessing fundamental valuation-related information out of the market. Therefore, regulatory attempts to enhance one of these two measures of allocative efficiency in *all* jurisdictions will seriously hinder efforts to enhance the other in *any* jurisdiction. Since market participants will differ in their relative preference for transparency and liquidity, there is no clear case to be made for precluding competition among market structures.

Social Efficiency

The allocative efficiency of our capital markets has increased dramatically over the past quarter century, but in and of itself this may tell us only that capital markets are becoming hyper-efficient casinos. It tells us very little about how well these markets are actually servicing the real economy.

Assuming we do not value capital markets for their casino services, we must evaluate their performance in terms of the ultimate social functions we may reasonably impute to them. Any notion of capital market 'social efficiency' would have to measure how cost effectively the markets allocate risks among investors with diverse preferences and abilities to bear risk, transform passive savings into economically productive investments, process and disseminate information from diverse sources, and provide an infrastructure for processing transactions.

The efficient markets hypothesis implicitly holds that maximal social efficiency necessarily results from market prices fully reflecting fundamental values, that it is trading in free and competitive markets that allows this to obtain, and that cheap and easy trading must therefore be at the root of social efficiency.

The operational efficiency of our capital markets having risen dramatically particularly over the last decade, the markets now bear a fair resemblance to the 'frictionless' markets of pure economic theory.[12] Cheap and easy trading means that there are no longer any significant time and cost barriers to even the shortest-term speculation, within or across national markets, and casual evidence suggests that such speculation is coming increasingly to dominate the operations of the markets.

If cheap and easy trading fuels speculation, we need to consider whether speculation might serve to drive market prices toward or away from fundamental values. A significant body of empirical evidence now exists which suggests that trading *itself* is a source of volatility in capital markets,[13] and specifically short-term speculative trading which acts to exacerbate trends rather than to correct deviations from fundamental values. Since short-term speculative trading strategies are not based on fundamental value considerations, any interventions which can effectively curb such trading will reduce the extent of price fluctuations about fundamental values. This in turn must reduce investment risk, increase the information content of market prices, more efficiently allocate capital among investment opportunities, and hence increase social efficiency.[14]

The more direct costs of supporting capital market activities must also not be overlooked. Summers and Summers (1990) estimated the private cost of operating the US securities markets at nearly one-quarter of total US corporate profits. Since, as James Tobin (1984) has emphasized, very little of the markets' activities have any direct relationship with the financing of real investment, governments are obliged to consider whether it is right for taxpayers to continue financing the underwriting and policing of each new private market which emerges. Governments are also obliged to consider the social opportunity costs of the enormous amount of private resources supporting capital market activity. The private gains from discerning that Mousetraps Inc. is 50% undervalued may be the same as those from boosting its value 50% through the actual design of a better mousetrap, but the social gains from the latter activity must be considerably higher.

The simplest and most effective way to curb the flow of private resources into short-term speculative trading, without unduly interfering with 'value investing', is to impose a transaction tax on trading.[15] Concerns that such a tax would significantly reduce market liquidity appear unwarranted, given the lack of evidence of such an effect from markets where the tax is now or once was in operation. International agreement on a minimum tax would prevent it being purged through regulatory arbitrage, and taxing on a residency rather than situs basis would reduce the attractiveness of diverting trading offshore. Revenues raised could be used to finance directly the market policing and underwriting activities required of government.

The United States repealed its transfer tax back in 1965, and the European Community is unfortunately moving toward the abolition of all forms of transfer tax within the Community. Politically, a harmonized minimum tax may therefore prove difficult to achieve. The relative ease with which it could be implemented, modified, and uniformly administered, however, makes this type of coordinated regulatory intervention a particularly sensible one to pursue.

3. Fairness

Sir Kenneth Berrill, the former Chairman of the UK Securities and Investments Board, nicely defined the fairness objective as 'protecting Aunt Agatha'. The 1982 UK Gower Report, covering the general area of investor protection, emphasized the importance many place on this objective in stating that a free and efficient market would 'not afford protection to investors which anyone today would regard as adequate'.[16]

As national boundaries become increasingly irrelevant to the operation of financial markets, protecting Aunt Agatha becomes increasingly difficult for national authorities. Deterring, detecting, and punishing fraud will undoubtedly require greater formal cooperation and coordination among national authorities than we have at present. This is where international organizations like the ICMG and IOSCO[17] should become increasingly important.

The objective of fairness in capital market operations, however, should never be considered grounds for seeking top-down harmonization. The costs of inadequate or misguided fairness-related regulation will only be borne by those falling under the jurisdiction of the responsible authority.

Protecting investors, or redistributing income among them through such means as commission controls, should remain issues for national authorities. National governments have a multitude of state-specific reasons for favouring particular equity-efficiency mixes in different markets, and there is nothing to be gained from mandating one blend over others across national jurisdictions.

It must be recognized that many types of regulations commonly considered to be fairness-related actually have serious implications for market efficiency (like insider trading laws in securities markets) or systemic risk (like deposit insurance schemes in retail financial markets). Whether imposed harmonization is appropriate must therefore depend on the criteria previously laid out for those two types of regulation.

Conclusions

The debate over the appropriate regulatory response to capital market globalization has, to date, been dominated by concerns over how best to achieve international harmonization of an ad hoc assortment of 'important' regulations. Market integration is not in and of itself, however, sufficient grounds for pursuing regulatory integration. In many cases, the competitive forces of international regulatory arbitrage are more likely to shape regulation which will foster the efficient and equitable operation of capital markets.

This essay has attempted first and foremost to lay the conceptual foundations for determining where a *prima facie* case can be made for some form of regulatory harmonization from above. Such foundations must be consistent with the fundamental rationale for capital market regulation: reducing *systemic risk*, fostering *market efficiency*, and promoting equity, or *fairness*, in market operation. While harmonized regulatory intervention can effectively address problems relating to systemic risk and market efficiency, deriving the appropriate form of intervention requires a greater appreciation than has hitherto been shown for the multiple sources of risk and dimensions of efficiency.

References

Bank for International Settlements, *Survey of Foreign Exchange Market Activity*, Basle, February 1990.

Bloch, Ernest, 'Multiple Regulators: Their Constituencies and Policies', in Yakov Amihud, Thomas S. Y. Ho, and Robert A. Schwartz (eds.), *Market Making and the Changing Structure of the Securities Industry*, Lexington, MA: Lexington Books, 1985.

Chapman, Alger B., 'International Securities Regulation in a Global Electronic Environment', in Daniel R. Siegel (ed.), *Innovation and Technology in the Markets*, Chicago: Probus, 1990.

French, Kenneth and Richard Roll, 'Stock Return Variances: The Arrival of Information and the Reaction of Traders', *Journal of Financial Economics* 17 (1986), pp. 5–26.

Gibson, Heather D., *The Eurocurrency Markets, Domestic Financial Policy and International Instability*. London: Macmillan 1989.

Gower, Jim, *Review of Investor Protection—A Discussion Document*. London: HMSO, 1982.

Hamilton, James L., 'Electronic Market Linkages and the Distribution of Order Flow: The Case of Off-Board Trading of NYSE-Listed Stocks', in Henry C. Lucas, Jr., and Robert A. Schwartz (eds.), *The Challenge of Information Technology for the Securities Markets*, Homewood, IL: Dow Jones-Irwin, 1989.

Kanda, Hideki, 'Systemic Risk and International Finance Markets', in Franklin R. Edwards and Hugh T. Patrick (eds.), *Regulating International Financial Markets: Issues and Policies*, Boston: Kluwer, 1992.

Kane, Edward J., 'Impact of Regulation on Economic Behavior', *Journal of Finance* 36 (May 1981), pp. 355-367.

Kane, Edward J., 'Tension Between Competition and Coordination in International Financial Regulation', in Catherine England (ed.), *Governing Banking's Future*, Boston: Kluwer, 1991.

Kane, Edward J., 'Government Officials as a Source of Systemic Risk in International Financial Markets', in Franklin R. Edwards and Hugh T. Patrick (eds.), *Regulating International Financial Markets: Issues and Policies*, Boston: Kluwer, 1992.

Kapstein, Ethan B., 'Supervising International Banks: Origins and Implications of the Basle Accord', *Essays in International Finance* 185 (December 1991), Princeton University.

Keynes, John Maynard, *The General Theory of Employment, Interest and Money*, London: Macmillan 1936.

Schaefer, Stephen, 'Financial Regulation: The Contribution of the Theory of Finance'. in John Fingleton (ed.), *The Internationalism of Capital Markets and the Regulatory Response*, London: Graham and Trotman, 1992.

Schwert, G. William, 'Why Does Stock Market Volatility Change Over Time'? *NBER Working Paper* (1988).

Shiller, Robert, 'Stock Prices and Social Dynamics', *Brookings Papers on Economic Activity* (1984:2), pp. 457–498.

Stiglitz, Joseph E., 'Using Tax Policy to Curb Speculative Short-Term Trading', *Journal of Financial Services Research* 3 (1989), pp. 101–115.

Summers, Lawrence H., and Victoria P. Summers, 'When Financial Markets Work Too Well: A Case for a Securities Transaction Tax', in Daniel R. Siegel (ed.), *Innovation and Technology in the Markets*, Chicago: Probus, 1990.

Tinic, S., and R. West, *Investing in Securities: An Efficient Markets Approach*, Reading, MA: Addison-Wesley, 1979.

Tobin, James, 'On the Efficiency of the Financial System', *Lloyds Bank Review* 153 (July 1984), pp. 1–15.

Notes

1 See Bloch (1985). The concept of the 'regulatory dialectic' was developed by Edward Kane. See Kane (1981) for a clear and elegant exposition.

2 *Credit Risk* refers to non-tradable assets, such as loans, while *position risk* refers to tradable securities. The 1988 Basle Accord on capital adequacy deals only with credit risk.

3 See Kapstein (1991) for interesting historical commentary.

4 See Schaefer (1992).

5 See Kane (1991).

6 See Schaefer (1992) for a full exposition of this problem.

7 See Kanda (1992).

8 See Chapman (1990).

9 See, for example, Kane (1992).

10 See Hamilton (1989).

11 See Gibson (1989) and Tinic and West (1979).

12 In 1989, the daily volume of global foreign exchange trading was approximately forty times the average daily volume of world trade (Bank for International Settlements, 1990).

13 See, for example, French and Roll (1986), Shiller (1984), and Schwert (1988).

14 See Summers and Summers (1990) for a clear and detailed exposition.

15 Such a tax was long ago proposed by Keynes (1936), and more recently by Tobin (1984), Stiglitz (1989), and Summers and Summers (1990).

16 Gower (1982, para. 5.13).

17 IOSCO = International Organization of Securities Commissions. ICMG = International Capital Markets Group, which consists of the Fédération Internationale des Bourses de Valeurs (Paris), the International Federation of Accountants (New York), and the International Bar Association Section on Business Law (London).

Rating the EC As An Optimal Currency Area: Is It Worse Than the US?

THIRD PRIZE

Summary

The viability of EMU has been questioned on the grounds that the loss of the exchange rate for adjustment purposes is not compensated by other instruments. This paper aims to assemble evidence on this issue taking the US as reference. The following indications emerge. Firstly, the economies of the EC countries are more homogenous than those of the US states and therefore less likely to experience asymmetric disturbances. Secondly, the exchange rate instrument is less efficient in the EC, because of the higher real wage rigidity and the scarce labour mobility within the EC states. Finally, powerful budgetary tools are available both in the EC and in the US to face asymmetric shocks.

Lorenzo Bini Smaghi is Head of division in the Research Department of the Banca d'Italia, Rome. A graduate of the Université Catholique de Louvain in 1978 he received his MA in Economics at the University of Southern California in 1980 and his Ph.D. in Economics from the University of Chicago in 1988. He has been an alternate member of the EC Monetary Committee and a member of the Foreign Exchange and of the Monetary Policy Subcommittees of the Committee of EC Central Bank Governors.

Silvia Vori is an economist in the Research Department of the Banca d'Italia, Rome. She graduated from the University of Rome in 1984 and undertook post graduate studies at the University of Michigan where she received an MA in 1987.

6

Rating The EC As An Optimal Currency Area: Is It Worse Than the US?

LORENZO BINI SMAGHI AND SILVIA VORI*

'In view of the apparent strength of the forces pushing Europe towards more integration, one wonders whether political leaders are simply ill-informed, whether they are assigning more weight to non-economic considerations than are the economists, or whether economic analysis is itself deficient in some ways.'

Ingram (1973), p. 2.

Introduction

In discussions of European economic and monetary union (EMU), a recurrent—and challenging—question is whether the European Community is an optimal currency area. The literature has recently re-opened this issue, most often reaching negative conclusions at a time, paradoxically, when major political decisions to move towards EMU have been taken. In fact, EC countries' authorities have already accepted that the exchange rate constraint became more and more binding, despite powerful external and internal shocks such as large swings in oil prices and in the exchange rate of the dollar or German unification. The apparent contradiction between economic reasoning and political decisions, pointed out by Ingram two decades ago, has not been addressed.

The aim of this paper is to throw some sand in the works and dis-arrange the apparently smooth, rational line of reasoning taken up in

* Acknowledgements: We wish to thank A. Liccardi for research assistance and V. D'Ambrosio for the editing. We are the only ones responsible for remaining errors and for opinions. Although the research is the result of a joint effort. L. Bini Smaghi is mainly responsible for the introduction and section 2, S. Vori for section 1 and the Appendix.

the recent optimal currency area literature, which can be summarized as follows: giving up the exchange rate as an instrument for adjustment to asymmetric shocks will entail major costs for European economies; EMU will therefore not be viable unless other instruments such as factor mobility or fiscal policy, become available.

Our objective is a limited one—not to make an overall assessment of the optimality of the EC as a currency area but to highlight some pieces of evidence that may call into question the underlying assumptions of this literature. Somewhat provocatively, we take the United States as a benchmark for the EC.[1] We are obviously aware of the limitations of such a comparison. The EC is not yet a currency union—in fact, the latest members have not yet fully liberalized trade and capital movements. The transition to a different exchange rate regime may bring about modifications of economic structures and of agents' behaviour; affecting the way in which economies respond to economic disturbances. The relevant comparison, if the data were available, would presumably be with the US at the start of its union; even then, other relevant differences would still distort the analysis.

Bearing these caveats in mind, the analysis of the EC and US economies lead to the following broad conclusions:

• the economies of the EC states, especially the founding members, are more homogenous than those of the various regions of the United States and are therefore less likely to be subject to asymmetric disturbances;

• in the EC, real wage rigidity is greater than in the US; therefore, *prima facie*, the exchange rate should be a less efficient instrument of adjustment to asymmetric shocks within the former than within the latter;

• in the EC, labour mobility within member states is as low as between member states; therefore the exchange rate does not represent an efficient instrument of adjustment within the EC;

• powerful budgetary instruments for adjustment to asymmetric shocks are available in the EC and the US; in the former they operate through stage budgets, in the latter through the federal budget.

The paper is organized in two sections. The first one examines the likelihood and relevance of asymmetric shocks and inquires whether the basic characteristics of the EC economies are such as to make exchange rate variations an efficient instrument of adjustment. The second section assesses labour mobility and budgetary policy as substitutes for the exchange rate.

1. The exchange rate as an instrument of adjustment

The exchange rate can be an instrument of adjustment to shocks that affect economies differently insofar as it favours the modification of the relative prices of goods produced in two economies. Therefore, the usefulness of the exchange rate depends on:
i) the extent to which the economies are subject to differential shocks;
ii) the extent to which the exchange rate can modify relative prices.

1.1 Asymmetry of shocks

Regions within a monetary area may be affected by different shocks that alter their relative performances. The extent to which regional economies have been affected by different shocks can be assessed by comparing their behaviour over time. We examined the correlation of each member state's GDP with GDP in the rest of the area, in terms of deviation from trend. The US and the EC are both considered: for the EC, the aggregates EC total, EC10 (ERM countries in 1991) and EC6 (founding countries) have been analyzed; for the US, the states have been regrouped according to the 12 Federal Reserve districts (Table 1; see also Tootell, 1990). The results (Table 2) suggest that the EC economies, in particular those of the founding members, move more uniformly than the US regions. This holds independently of the time period: the average correlation is .95 for the original EC in the 1963–89 period (.96 in 1979–89), .69 for the US (.66 in 1979–89).[2]

This simple correlation analysis cannot discriminate between demand and supply shocks or between shocks and responses (Bayoumi and Eichengreen, 1992).[3] The higher correlation between GDP movements within the EC may be partly due to the past use of autonomous responses in the member states, such as exchange rate modifications, to absorb the impact of differentiated shocks.

To address this issue the distinction can be made between shocks affecting individual regions, such as an earthquake or a wage push, and shocks impinging on all the regions but with a variable intensity because of structural differences—a good instance being an oil shock.

Table 1 Main indicators for EC States and US Federal Reserve districts – 1989(1)

EC State			FED district		
Belgium	GDP = 153.0 (% EC GDP: 3.2) Population = 9.9 GDP per capita = 15.5		FED1 = Connecticut, Maine, New Hampshire, Massachusetts, Rhode Island, Vermont	GDP = 311.9 (% US GDP: 6.1) Population = 13.0 GDP per capita = 24.0	
Denmark	GDP = 104.7 (% EC GDP: 2.2) Population = 5.1 GDP per capita = 20.5		FED2 = New York	GDP = 441.1 (% US GDP: 8.6) Population = 18.0 GDP per capita = 24.5	
France	GDP = 958.2 (% EC GDP: 19.7) Population = 56.2 GDP per capita = 17.0		FED3 = Pennsylvania, New Jersey, Delaware	GDP = 446.7 (% US GDP: 8.7) Population = 20.4 GDP per capita = 22.0	
Germany	GDP = 1189.1 (% EC GDP: 24.5) Population = 62.0 GDP per capita = 19.2		FED4 = Ohio	GDP = 211.5 (% US GDP: 4.1) Population = 10.9 GDP per capita = 19.4	
Greece	GDP = 54.2 (% EC GDP: 1.1) Population = 10.0 GDP per capita = 5.4		FED5 = Virginia, West Virginia, Maryland, North Carolina, South Carolina	GDP = 453.7 (% US GDP: 8.9) Population = 22.7 GDP per capita = 20.0	
Ireland	GDP = 33.9 (% EC GDP: 0.7) Population = 3.5 GDP per capita = 9.7		FED6 = Tennessee, Mississippi, Louisiana, Georgia, Alabama, Florida	GDP = 634.2 (% US GDP: 12.4) Population = 35.2 GDP per capita = 18.0	
Italy	GDP = 865.8 (% EC GDP: 17.8) Population = 57.5 GDP per capita = 15.1		FED7 = Wisconsin, Michigan, Iowa, Indiana, Illinois	GDP = 690.2 (% US GDP: 13.5) Population = 34.2 GDP per capita = 20.2	

	GDP	Population	GDP per capita		GDP	Population	GDP per capita
Luxembourg	= 7.0 (% EC GDP: 0.1)	= 0.4	= 17.5	FED8 = Kentucky, Missouri, Arkansas	= 203.1 (% US GDP: 3.9)	= 11.3	= 18.0
Netherlands	= 223.7 (% EC GDP: 4.6)	= 14.9	= 15.0	FED9 = Montana, North Dakota, South Dakota, Minnesota	= 129.0 (% US GDP: 2.5)	= 6.5	= 19.8
Portugal	= 45.3 (% EC GDP: 0.9)	= 9.8	= 4.6	FED10 = Wyoming, Nebraska, Kansas, Colorado, Oklahoma	= 209.6 (% US GDP: 4.1)	= 11.1	= 18.9
Spain	= 380.0 (% EC GDP: 7.8)	= 33.9	= 11.2	FED11 = New Mexico, Texas	= 365.5 (% US GDP: 7.1)	= 18.5	= 19.8
U. Kingdom	= 837.5 (% EC GDP: 17.3)	= 57.2	= 14.6	FED12 = Washington, Oregon, Idaho, Nevada, California, Utah, Arizona, Alaska, Hawaii	= 1028.8 (% US GDP: 20.0)	= 45.7	= 22.5
EC(2)	= 4852.4 (4752.9) (3396.8)	= 320.4 (300.6) (200.9)	= 15.1 (15.8) (16.9)	USA (3)	= 5125.3	= 247.5	= 20.7

Source: OECD, Bureau of Economic Analysis (BRA), US Department of Commerce.
(1) Data at current prices and exchange rates. GDP is measured in billion dollars; population in millions; GDP per capita in thousands dollars.
(2) Data in the first parenthesis refer to the EC10, in the second parenthesis to EC6.
(3) The total does not include the District of Columbia.

Table 2 Correlation of real GDP between states and rest of area (1)

	BLEU	F	D :	I	NL	DK	IRL	E	UK	P	GR	Mean	Variance
EC 1963–89	.97	.95	.91	.91	.97	.71	.81	.93	.29*	.95	.95	.85	.04
1979–89	.93	.83	.96	.87	.94	.15*	.90	.87	−.15*	.90	.89	.74	.14
EC10 1963–89	.96	.94	.91	.90	.97	.71	.81	.92	.29*			.83	.05
1979–89	.91	.79	.96	.85	.94	.15*	.90	.88	−.14*			.69	.16
EC6 1963–89	.97	.97	.91	.95	.97							.95	.001
1979–89	.98	.95	.93	.99	.98							.96	.001

	FED1	FED2	FED3	FED4	FED5	FED6	FED7	FED8	FED9	FED10	FED11	FED12	Mean	Variance
USA 1963–89	.49	.66	.83	.97	.93	.79	.91	.98	.64	.16*	.10*	.78	.69	.09
1979–89	.70	.72	.84	.99	.93	.90	.99	.98	.45*	−.27*	−.30*	.96	.66	.22

Source: EUROSTAT, BEA, US Department of Commerce.
(1) Correlation between the States' Real per capital GDP (deviation from trend) and the rest of area Real per capita GDP (deviation from trend). The coefficients are all significant at .01 level, except those marked by an asterisk.

The two types of shock may be termed, respectively, state-specific and sector-specific.

We have examined the extent to which the behaviour of EC economies can be explained by sector-specific or state-specific factors, using a methodology developed by Stockman (1987).[4] The analysis concentrates on manufacturing production. Table 3 shows the proportion of the variance in EC manufacturing output explained by sector-specific and state-specific factors.

Considering the founding members of the EC, from 1976 to 1990 over 60 per cent of the variance explained by both factors as a whole is accounted for by sector-specific factors, 15 per cent by state-specific factors, and the remainder by the interaction of the two. For the period

Table 3 State and sector specific components of manufacturing production variability (1)

	state SS	sector SS	R^2	total SS	explained SS	state and sector SS
A. Period 1976–90						
EC	4.36	3.90	.795	23.35	18.55	9.30
	(3.69)	(3.96)				
EC10	2.63	2.99	.803	16.08	12.90	6.69
	(3.53)	(4.13)				
EC6	.49	2.14	.805	4.40	3.54	3.29
	(2.54)	(6.32)				
USA(2)	1.56	19.23	.902	33.32	30.05	27.01
	(2.40)	(31.87)				
B. Period 1981–90						
EC	1.56	1.34	.716	9.54	6.83	3.58
	(3.16)	(2.67)				
EC10	.96	1.28	.711	6.11	4.34	2.78
	(3.51)	(3.76)				
EC6	.15	.83	.777	2.44	1.90	1.53
	(2.05)	(4.03)				
USA(2)	.78	9.08	.899	19.70	17.70	13.08
	(1.58*)	(30.40)				

(1) SS = sum of squares. See the appendix for the methodology and data description.
In parenthesis are the F statistics, all significant at the .01 level, except that marked by an asterisk, which is significant at the .05 level.
Luxembourg is excluded from EC aggregates.
(2) For the USA the last available data refer to 1989.

1981–1990 the weight of the state-specific factors falls to 10 per cent. Considering the broader group of EC countries, the share of production variance explained by both factors which is due to sector-specific factors is about 40 per cent. The corresponding exercise for US Federal Reserve districts shows that about 70 per cent of the variance explained by the two different components can be attributed to sector-specific factors; state-specific factors accounted for 6 per cent.

Interestingly, for all EC countries except Ireland there is a significant inverse correlation between sector-specific and state-specific factors (Table 4). In the US, several regions show positive correlations and only two significant negative coefficients in the longer interval; only one significant negative coefficient is reported for 1981–1989. This suggests that, while in the EC state-specific factors tend to offset the effects of sector-specific factors, in the US the former tend to compound the latter.

The national impact of sectoral factors depends on the sectoral composition of an economy's output. On average, the differences between regional production structures are much larger within the US than within the EC.[5] The correlation between EC states' indices of manufacturing production, net of the state-specific disturbances shown in Table 3, is on average close to 1 and higher than the corresponding one computed for the US regions.

This evidence suggests that EC economies are more similar and tend to behave more as a group than US regions and are therefore less likely to suffer from asymmetric shocks.[6] This would suggest that the exchange rate is a less useful instrument of adjustment in the EC than it would be in the US.

Of course, this result is based on the present structure of the EC economies. Economic and monetary union could promote increased specialization, with EC countries becoming as highly specialized as US regions. According to Krugman (1992), a reduction in transaction costs, whether these costs take the form of transportation expenses, tariffs or regulation disparities, would increase the probability of external economies leading to geographical concentration of an industry. According to Emerson et al. (1990), however, the removal of barriers tends to spur intra-industry integration, which would make the effects of sector-specific shocks more uniform.

Whether the 'peripheral' members are specializing in the same sectors as the founders is an interesting line of research.[7] The data suggest that foreign direct investment in Portugal and Spain is apparently

Table 4 Correlation between state and sector-specific factors of manufacturing production variability (1)

		B	F	D	I	NL	DK	IRL	E	UK	P	GR
EC	1976–90	-.823	-.888	-.801	-.770	-.868	-.651	-.422*	-.766	-.497	-.726	-.832
	1981–90	-.872	-.885	-.798	-.733	-.844	-.595	-.478*	-.705	-.839	-.921	-.909
EC10	1976–90	-.827	-.887	-.798	-.772	-.871	-.653	-.440*	-.761	-.498		
	1981–90	-.877	-.887	-.803	-.735	-.848	-.595	-.511*	-.698	-.840		
EC6	1976–90	-.828	-.893	-.797	-.770	-.871						
	1981–90	-.885	-.893	-.809	-.734	-.853						

		FED1	FED2	FED3	FED4	FED5	FED6	FED7	FED8	FED9	FED10	FED11	FED12
USA	1976–89	-.368*	-.800	-.626	.538	.001*	.226*	.541	.567	.150*	-.357*	-.258*	-.195*
	1981–89	-.172*	-.799	-.371*	.303*	.075*	.073*	.516*	.350*	-.178*	-.103*	-.247*	-.229*

(1) Correlation between the percentage change of two different indices of manufacturing production, built as the weighted sum of the estimated indices relative to single sectors of production obtained by fitting the model described in the appendix first considering only the sector-specific component, then only the state-specific component.
Luxembourg is excluded from EC aggregates.
The coefficients are all significant at .05 level, except those marked by an asterisk.

concentrated in sectors in which these countries are relatively less specialized, such as finance, insurance and real estate in Portugal and
manufacturing in Spain. In such sectors as agriculture and tourism,
whose share of GDP is higher in Portugal and Spain than in the EC,
foreign direct investment is relatively limited.

In short, it appears that within the EC factors other than transportation
costs play an important role in determining industrial location.[8] One such
factor might be the greater population density and the higher cost of land
(compared with the US), which impede the concentration of industry in
certain areas. Other reasons could be Europe's lower labour mobility,
discussed below, which limits the possibilities of concentration.

In summary, the evidence suggests that thanks to its economic structure the EC should be less subject to asymmetric productivity shocks
than is the US. Other things being equal, therefore, the exchange rate is
presumably a less useful instrument of adjustment in the former than it
would be in the latter. Other types of shocks, restricted to a specific
area might occur, such as an earthquake, or the recent example of
German unification. Arguments can be made in favour of maintaining
the possibility of using the exchange rate to adjust to these shocks,
although presumably other instruments have been used as in the case
of German unification.

1.2 Effectiveness of the exchange rate instrument

Jones and Corden (1976) emphasized that a change in the exchange
rate cannot produce switching effects if real wages are sticky. If unions
negotiate on the basis of real wages, i.e. if agents have no money illusion, the exchange rate cannot modify relative prices. The effectiveness of a variation in the exchange rate thus depends on the presence of
nominal wage rigidity and the absence of real wage rigidity.

Real wage rigidity can be assessed on the basis of the elasticity of
nominal wages with respect to: i) prices and ii) excess supply or
demand in the labour markets. The higher is the first elasticity with
respect to the second, the less effective is the exchange rate as an
instrument for modifying relative prices. If wages are highly indexed
but are responsive to unemployment, adjustment in a region negatively
affected by a shock will not be possible through a devaluation but will
take place through a temporary rise in unemployment. On the contrary
if wages are little sensitive to unemployment and are not indexed,
adjustment can be attained through a devaluation.

Table 5 reports estimates of elasticities of wages with respect to prices and unemployment from OECD (1989). These measures differ among EC countries, but for all responsiveness of wages to prices is higher than to unemployment.[9] In the US and Japan, on the contrary, the elasticity of the real wage with respect to prices is larger than that with respect to unemployment.[10] The ratio of the two elasticities, which represents the real wage rigidity, is greater than unity in all European countries, particularly in Germany, even though indexation is forbidden.

Table 5 Real wage rigidity

Countries	Elasticity of nominal wage with respect to:		Index of real wage rigidity
	Prices	Unemployment rate	
	(a)	(b)	$-(a)/(b)$
Belgium	.25	−.25	1.0
Denmark	.25	−.10	2.5
France	.50	−.29	1.7
Germany	.75	−.11	6.8
Italy	.60	−.39	1.5
Netherlands	.50	−.27	1.9
Spain	.25	−.20	1.3
U.K.	.33	−.15	2.2
USA	.14	−.61	.22
Canada	.18	−.51	.35
Japan	.66	−1.87	.35

Source: Calculations based on OECD (1989).

The degree of wage flexibility could change with the increasing integration of Community goods and labour markets, eventually if EMU were accompanied by more centralized wage negotiations. However, if real wage rigidity continues to be larger in the EC countries, the exchange rate will be a less effective instrument for adjustment than in would be in the US.

2. Alternative Instruments

The literature has concentrated on two main instruments that are expected to compensate for the renunciation of exchange rate flexibility: labour mobility and fiscal policy.

2.1 Labour mobility

Mundell (1961) pointed to the importance of labour mobility as an instrument of adjustment in a fixed exchange rate system. Direct evidence on labour mobility is rather difficult to assemble. A study by the OECD (1986) concluded that mobility within the US is two or three times greater than mobility between European states. Eichengreen (1990b) found that the dispersion of rates of unemployment is about twice as high in the EC as in the US. The data shown in Table 6 confirm these results. The coefficient of variation of unemployment rates within the founding members of the EC is about twice that within the US; for the entire EC the dispersion is four times higher.

Eichengreen also attempted to estimate the speed of adjustment of labour markets in various countries. His results confirm that labour markets adjust more quickly to disturbances in the US than in the EC, although not substantially (adjustment is about 25 per cent faster in the US). This seems to be due to the barriers to labour mobility within the EC, including cultural and language differences.

Table 6 Unemployment rates (percentage points)

		Mean	Variance	C. V.(1)	Maximum	Minimum	Difference
EC	1983	10.91	8.89	.27	17.0	7.8	9.2
	1990	8.93	12.03	.39	15.9	4.6	11.3
EC10	1983	11.60	8.20	.25	17.0	8.2	8.8
	1990	9.55	12.07	.36	15.9	5.5	10.4
EC6	1983	10.14	4.92	.22	13.2	8.2	5.0
	1990	8.45	2.94	.20	10.8	6.2	4.6
USA	1983	9.28	3.03	.19	12.2	6.8	5.4
	1990	5.43	0.33	.11	6.2	4.6	1.6

Sources: OECD, US Dept. of Labor.
Luxembourg is excluded from EC aggregates.

While the completion of the internal market is bound to reduce the barriers to labour mobility, it is most unlikely that the sort of labour market integration prevailing in the US can be replicated in the EC in the foreseeable future. However, if labour mobility is limited even within countries, the exchange rate will have little effect in adjusting to asymmetric shocks. In short, international labour mobility cannot substitute for the exchange rate instrument if internal labour mobility is lacking.[11]

Table 7 reports data on the dispersion of unemployment rates within the EC countries. Interestingly, internal dispersion increased in all countries during the eighties, regardless of the trend in the national rate. Comparing the data of Tables 6 and 7, it can be seen that dispersion of unemployment rates is greater within Italy, Spain and the UK than among EC countries; dispersion in Germany, France and the Netherlands is lower, but still at least as high as between the founding members of the EC.[12] Following Mundell's analysis these countries are poor candidates for flexible exchange rates.

A further consideration should be given to the welfare costs of labour mobility. In Mundell's analysis, labour mobility does not affect a nation's welfare, which is assumed to depend only on inflation and unemployment. The fact that labour is not mobile within countries, and that even large inter-regional unemployment disparities persist without inducing equilibrating labour migration, indicates that this assumption may be a gross simplification.[13] In the major European countries, migration is not considered a desirable means of adjustment as it entails social and economic costs that economists generally ignore. This is also reflected in the EC's policy on immigration from the rest of the world. Though this issue is clearly beyond the scope of the present work, this attitude strongly suggests that the lack of labour mobility is not seen as an obstacle to EMU and that adjustment would be achieved by other means.[14] In particular, regional policies to attract investment to areas hurt by shocks already play an important role in the EC and will become even more important in EMU.

2.2 Fiscal policy

The literature has emphasized the role of fiscal policy in ensuring the viability of a currency union,[15] but we need to distinguish between the stabilization, redistribution and allocation functions of fiscal policy. The relevant one for adjustment to asymmetric shocks is stabilization.

Table 7 Regional unemployment rates (percentage points)

	Mean	Variance	C. V.(1)	Maximum	Minimum	Difference
W. Germany						
1983	7.47	3.42	.25	10.8	4.4	6.4
1990	6.12	4.85	.36	10.4	3.0	7.4
France						
1983	7.93	2.23	.19	10.2	5.8	4.4
1990	9.08	3.33	.20	11.8	6.7	5.1
Italy						
1983	9.35	10.71	.35	16.1	5.8	10.3
1990	11.02	45.22	.61	21.0	3.3	17.7
Netherlands						
1983	12.60	3.50	.15	14.0	9.9	4.1
1990	8.43	2.91	.20	10.9	7.2	3.7
Spain						
1983	14.50	28.07	.37	22.5	10.1	12.4
1990	16.04	40.67	.40	29.8	7.4	22.4
UK						
1983	12.13	8.54	.24	16.8	8.2	8.6
1990	8.05	13.35	.45	17.1	4.2	12.9

Source: EUROSTAT.
(1) Coefficient of
Variation
List of Regions:

W. Germany
Schleswig-Holstein
Hamburg
Niedersachsen
Bremen
Nordrhein-Westfalen
Hassen
Rheinland-Pfalz
Baden-Wuerttemberg
Bayern
Saarland
Berlin (West)

Netherlands
Noord-Nederland
Oost-Nederland
West-Nederland
Zuid-Nederland

France
Ile de France
Bassin Parisien
Nord-Pas-de-Calais
Est
Ouest
Sud-Ouest
Centre-Est
Mediterranée

Spain
Galicia
Asturias
Cantabria
Pais Vasco
Navarra
Rioja
Aragon
Castilla-Leon
Castilla-La Mancha
Extremadura
Cataluna
Comunidad Valenciana
Balearas
Andalucia

Italy
Nord Ovest
Lombardia
Nord Est
Emilia-Romagna
Centro
Lazio
Campania
Abruzzi-Molise
Sud
Sicilia
Sardegna

UK
North
Yorkshire and Humberside
East Midlands
East Anglia
South East
South West
West Midlands
North West
Wales
Scotland
Northern Ireland

Sachs and Sala-i-Martin (1991) examined the role played by the US federal budget in compensating for changes in states' relative income. In a US state adversely affected by a shock, disposable income is sustained by a reduction in the proportion of taxes paid to the federal government and by direct transfers in the form of federal grants-in-aid. Other federal expenditures, such as interest payments and military outlays, are not considered as forms of income support that can foster the adjustment to asymmetric shocks.[16] Sachs and Sala-i-Martin found that on average about 35 per cent of change in states' relative income is offset through the federal tax system. Furthermore, federal grants-in-aid are correlated with relative income with a coefficient of 22 per cent. On the basis of the average tax and transfer to states, the elasticity of personal disposable income with respect to personal income is about 40 per cent. Hence the fraction of the initial shock absorbed by the federal fiscal system is about 40 per cent. The authors argued that EMU could be at risk if it failed to envisage some comparable federal shock absorber mechanism.

However, the findings of Sachs and Sala-i-Martin are open to a number of critical observations.

One objection concerns the empirical analysis. Von Hagen (1991) pointed out that federal tax receipts are related to the level of income, not to changes in states' relative income. Correcting for this effort, the proportion of the disposable income change offset by the federal tax system falls to just 8 per cent. Federal grants-in-aid are also correlated with income level rather than changes in relative personal income, suggesting that the US federal budget plays an important role in income redistribution but a much more limited one than often claimed in relative income stabilization.

A second objection is that the analysis concentrates on the US federal budget and ignores the state and local public finances. In 1991 state and local receipts and expenditures amounted to about 40 per cent of total general government spending, so their impact is substantial indeed.[17] Every state but Vermont has either statutory or constitutional balanced budget requirements, although the restrictions are not all equally binding.[18] A balanced budget requirement is bound to produce a procyclical policy, exacerbating the effects of asymmetric shocks, as recent research tends to demonstrate.[19]

Two additional pieces of evidence point in the same direction. An often ignored fact is that US unemployment insurance is largely administered at the state, not the federal, level. It is funded largely by corporate taxes. Benefit levels and eligibility criteria vary among states according to specific laws. Furthermore, 'the financing structure of the unemployment insurance programme levies higher taxes on companies with histories of sizeable layoffs' (Council of Economic Advisers, 1992, p. 106). In states affected by adverse shocks the increase in unemployment often gives rise to budget difficulties, which may prompt higher taxes or a reduction in unemployment benefits, exacerbating the macroeconomic effects of the shock and presumably providing an incentive for migration.[20]

Second, as was noted in section 1.1 (Table 4), for many US areas there is a positive correlation between the state-specific and the sector-specific factors in output variability. Since state fiscal policy can be taken as one of the main state-specific factors influencing income, this finding indicates that state budget have played little role in countering sector-specific disturbances.

Overall, when appropriate methodology is adopted the inter-state stabilization role of US budgetary policy seems to be more limited than is generally believed. Atkeson and Bayoumi (1991) found that no more than 13 per cent of a change in relative personal income is counteracted by US fiscal policy. They also found that the protection against income fluctuation provided by EC states is comparable to that offered in the US. In principle, therefore, as recognized by Mussa (1991), the EC has the tools to counter asymmetric shocks. However, the EMU Treaty limits, with some flexibility, government deficits to 3 per cent of national product.[21] The ability of member states to perform the desired stabilization function in the face of adverse shocks will therefore largely depend on their disciplined behaviour in favourable years.

The difference between income stabilization in the face of asymmetric shocks in the US and the EC concerns the level of government at which it is performed. The issue is whether one system is preferable to the other. The prevailing view within the EC seems to have shifted from advocacy of the centralized approach (McDougall, 1977) to acceptance of a more decentralized one, based on the principle of subsidiarity (Padoa-Schioppa *et al.*, 1987). Scholarly views also differ as arguments are raised in favour and against both systems. Indeed, several monetary unions, such as Switzerland or Belgium and Luxembourg, have done without a federal budget responsible for stabilization, and the US federal budget played no major role before 1929.[22]

This debate goes beyond the scope of this work. An interesting aspect on which greater attention should be devoted is the relationship between the integration of labour markets and the centralization of fiscal policy. Allen (1976) argued that one reason for centralizing fiscal policy is to prevent labour mobility from high-tax to the high-spending regions from undermining the stabilization function of regional fiscal policy and providing budget crises. If labour mobility within the EC increases or wage negotiations tend to be conducted increasingly at a centralized level, stabilization policy might be more efficiently conducted at the centralized level.

The above discussion has concentrated on the performance of the stabilization function through budgetary policy in the face of asymmetric shocks, which are the most disruptive to monetary unions. However, the Union may experience symmetric shocks, affecting all countries similarly, and therefore want to engineer a common budgetary policy response. In a centralized system the homogeneity of the budgetary response across states is guaranteed; in a decentralized system, strong forms of cooperation will be needed to overcome the externalities resulting from cross-border budgetary effects.[23]

Finally, some authors have argued that a viable monetary union also requires income redistribution between regions.[24] Such a redistribution would occur mainly through budget centralization, the establishment of uniform criteria for levying taxes and allocating transfers, precluding a situation in which regional governments can constantly evaluate their respective costs and benefits from the programme. However, as Allen (1976) recognized, redistribution requires a Union-wide welfare function, which itself can only be formulated by a political union.

In advocating a greater role for redistributive policies in the EC the McDougall report (1977) indicated in the 3–10 per cent range generally observed in monetary union the target for the ratio of net transfers from the EC to recipient regions.[25] Others, such as Eichengreen (1990a), indicated the US system of federal grants-in-aid, which amount to 2.7 per cent of GDP in 1991, as the model to follow for the EC.

We do not intend to discuss the validity of these arguments, but only to point out that the Community redistributive policies are much more important than is generally perceived. The data reported in Tables 8 and 9 show that although in 1990 per capita transfers in the US averaged 481 dollars, twice as much as in the EC (223 dollars), the variance is much lower in the former (8455 dollars across US states against 45,059 dollars in the EC). The US federal budget makes large transfers to all states, including the richer ones. On the contrary, the EC budget

Table 8 Distribution of US federal grants-in-aid

| | Grants (1) | | Grants in relation to: | | | | | |
| | | | Total US grants (2) | | State Personal Income (2) | | State Population (3) | |
	1981	1990	1981	1990	1981	1990	1981	1990
FED1	4.1	7.2	6.0	6.1	2.8	2.5	327	544
FED2	6.7	12.9	9.8	10.9	3.2	3.2	378	717
FED3	5.1	9.2	7.5	7.8	2.2	2.2	257	454
FED4	2.5	4.8	3.6	4.0	2.2	2.5	229	439
FED5	6.1	9.5	9.0	8.0	3.0	2.3	294	415
FED6	8.3	15.3	12.3	12.9	2.8	2.6	267	434
FED7	9.8	14.6	14.4	12.3	2.6	2.3	288	429
FED8	3.1	4.7	4.6	4.0	3.1	2.7	287	425
FED9	2.3	3.7	3.4	3.1	3.5	3.2	371	570
FED10	3.0	4.9	4.4	4.1	2.5	2.5	282	443
FED11	3.6	7.3	5.3	6.2	2.1	2.4	225	392
FED12	13.3	24.3	19.6	20.5	2.9	2.6	344	516
Mean	5.7	9.9	8.3	8.3	2.7	2.6	296	481
Variance	11.4	36.2	24.8	25.9	0.2	0.1	2554	8455

Sources: US Department of Commerce, BEA and Bureau of the Census.
(1) Billions of dollars
(2) Percentage points.
(3) Dollars per capita.

makes transfers mostly to poorer states. In 1990, per capita transfers to Germany amounted to 96 dollars, those to Ireland 822, Portugal 133, Greece 381. The transfers to Ireland are as large as those to the poorest US states. Those to Portugal and Greece are smaller but have increased by 100 and 50 per cent, respectively, since their admission to the EC (in 1986 and 1984). Net transfers to Ireland and Greece amount to 7 and 5 per cent of their GDP. These numbers are similar or close to those advocated in the McDougall report.

There are no doubts that budgetary issues will be the subject of increasing discussions as the EC moves towards EMU. Plans have already been agreed to restructure and to further increase the amounts distributed by EC budget in the next few years. This however might

Table 9 Distribution of Community budgetary payments and receipts

	Payments in relation to:						Receipts in relation to:					
	Total Payments		State Personal Income (1)		State Population (2)		Total Receipts (1)		State Personal Income (1)		State Population (1)	
	1981	1990	1981	1990	1981	1990	1981	1990	1981	1990	1981	1990
B	3.9	2.7	0.7	0.7	68	126	5.5	4.3	1.2	1.3	112	225
DK	3.7	3.2	1.3	1.4	125	297	2.0	1.9	0.8	0.9	77	192
D	16.1	13.0	0.5	0.5	46	97	28.1	25.0	0.9	1.0	91	209
GR	2.5	8.2	2.1	6.4	46	381	1.4	1.4	1.4	1.2	29	71
E	...	14.6	...	1.6	...	176	...	8.9	...	1.1	...	120
F	22.5	17.0	0.8	0.8	71	142	19.4	19.5	0.8	1.0	71	182
IRL	4.6	6.1	5.1	8.5	232	822	0.9	0.9	1.1	1.4	51	134
I	18.1	15.4	0.9	0.8	56	125	14.0	14.7	0.8	0.8	50	135
L	0.1	0.04	0.2	0.2	26	49	0.1	0.2	0.7	0.9	82	250
NL	8.3	8.1	1.1	1.5	100	254	7.1	6.3	1.1	1.3	100	223
P	...	3.0	...	2.5	...	133	...	1.2	...	1.1	...	61
UK	20.2	8.6	0.8	0.5	61	70	21.5	15.8	1.0	1.6	77	145
Mean	10.0	8.3	1.4	2.1	83	223	10.0	8.3	1.0	1.1	74	162
Variance	69.4	31.5	2.0	6.8	3540	45059	101.3	71.0	0.05	0.06	632	3726

Source: EC Official Journal, various issues.
(1) Percentage points.
(2) Dollars per capita.

not result in a greater centralization of budgetary policy until more decisive steps are taken towards political union.

Appendix

To assess the relative importance of sector-specific and state-specific components of industrial production we estimate, as in Stockman (1987), a statistical model:

$$d \ln \text{IP} (i,s,t) = m(i,s) + f(i,t) + g(s,t) + u(i,s,t)$$
$$i = \text{industry } s = \text{state } t = \text{time}$$

which allows to disaggregate the variance in the growth rate of the index of industrial production (*ip*) for a number of countries into three main components:

1 $m(i,s)$ is the average output growth in industry i in state s;

2 $f(i,t)$ represents the component of output growth common to sector i, for time t, across countries;

3 $g(s,t)$ represents the component of output growth common to state s, for time t, across sectors.

$u(i,s,t)$ is an idiosyncratic disturbance to sector i in state s at time t, assumed to be an *i.i.d.* random variable.

The industry effect is intended to account for disturbances to production functions, input prices, or product demand that would affect production in sector i and are common across states. The state effect represent state-specific disturbances, such as changes in policy, that affect output differently in different countries.

Estimation of the model is performed using OLS; $m(i,s)$ is a constant term specific to industry i in state s; $f(i,t)$ is a vector of dummy variables specific to industry i and to time t but common to all states; $g(s,t)$ is a vector of dummy variables specific to state s and to time t but common to all industries.

The parameters of the model can be identified through a set of normalizations. We chose to set $g(s^*,t)=0$ for one specific nation: in the case of estimation for the EC countries, the US has been taken as benchmark. The state effects for the other countries can be interpreted as the difference between the state-specific components of industrial output variation in state s and in the US. The time varying sector effect must also be interpreted relative to this normalization. The vector $f(i,t)$ estimates the industry-specific components of output growth in the benchmark country; in essence, this compensates for the zero coefficient on the state-specific components for the benchmark country. The second normalization implies that the estimated vectors $f(i,t)$ and $g(s,t)$ must be interpreted relative to the first time period (e.g., 1976 or 1981, depending on the time range of the estimation). Differences in output growth across industries and nations in the first period are reflected in the estimated constant terms $m(i,s)$. Estimation for the US regions was also performed relative to the whole US taken as normalization.

The results reported in Table 3 refer to estimation of the model with data on indices of industrial production for the following 11 sectors (in parenthesis, the ISIC division number):

1) food, beverages and tobacco (031);
2) textiles, clothing and leather (032);
3) wood and wood products (033);
4) paper and paper products (034);
5) chemicals and chemical products (035);
6) non metallic mineral products (036);
7) basic metals (037);
8) metal products, except machinery and equipment (381);
9) machinery, except electrical (382);
10) electrical machinery (383);
11) transport equipment (384).

Estimation was performed for the EC countries (Luxembourg is excluded from all aggregates due to lack of complete data) regrouped in three different aggregates (EC, EC10 and EC6) for the period 1976–90 and 1981–90; data source is OECD. For the 12 US Federal Reserve districts, we used data on State GDP, disaggregated according to the same classification above, made available by the BEA, US Department of Commerce.

In the Table we report the total sum of squares, the sum of squares explained by the model and the sum of squares attributable to the sector and the state factors taken together. Since the state- and sector-specific effects, $f(i)$ and $g(s)$, are correlated, in the first two columns we report the fractions of the output growth variations explained by the orthogonal components of f and g.

In Table 4 we computed the correlation between the state- and sector-specific components of manufacturing production variability. To do so, we built two different estimated indices of aggregate manufacturing production for each country; these have been computed considering for each observation first only the sector-specific estimated components of the model fitted to explain manufacturing output growth, then only the state-specific estimated components, and weighing them according to the relative weights of each sector in manufacturing output composition in the reference year (1985; the weights are from OECD).

References

Allen, P. R. (1976), 'Organization and Administration of a Monetary Union', Princeton Studies in International Finance, No. 38.

Atkeson, A., Bayoumi, T. (1991) 'Do Private Capital Markets Insure Against Risk in a Common Currency Area? Evidence from the United States'. mimeo, July.

Bayoumi, T., Eichengreen, B. (1992), 'Shocking Aspects of European Monetary Unification', Paper presented at the International Conference 'The Transition to Economic and Monetary Union in Europe', Banco de Portugal and CEPR, January.

Bertola, G. (1992), 'Models of Economic Integration and Localized Growth', Paper presented at the International Conference 'The Transition to Economic and Monetary Union in Europe', Banco de Portugal and CEPR, January.

Bruno, M., Sachs, J. D. (1985), 'Economics of Worldwide Stagflation', Basil Blackwell Ltd., Oxford.

Buiter, W., Kletzer, K. (1990), 'Reflection on the Fiscal Implications of a Common Currency', CEPR Discussion Paper, No. 418, May.

Coe, D. (1985), 'Nominal Wage, the NAIRU and Wage Flexibility', OECD Economic Studies, No. 5, Autumn, pp. 87–126.

Cohen, D., Wyplosz, C. (1989), 'The European Monetary Union: An Agnostic Evaluation', CEPR Discussion Paper No. 4306.

Council of Economic Advisers (1992), 'Economic Report of the President', Washington, D.C.

De Grauwe, P., Van Haverbeke, W. (1991), 'Is Europe an Optimum Currency Area? Evidence from Regional Data', CEPR Discussion Paper No. 555, May.

Eichengreen, B. (1990a), 'Currency Union', Economic Policy, April.

Eichengreen, B. (1990b), 'Is Europe an Optimum Currency Area?' CEPR Discussion Paper No. 478, November.

Emerson, M. et al. (1990), 'One Market, One Money', European Economy No. 44, October.

Ingram, J. C. (1973), 'The Case for European Monetary Integration', Princeton University Essays in International Finance, No. 98, April.

Inman, R., Rubinfeld, D. (1991), 'Fiscal Federalism in Europe. Lessons from the United States Experience', NBER Working Paper No. 3941.

Jones, R., Corden, M. (1976), 'Devaluation, Non-flexible Prices, and the Trade Balance for a Small Country', Canadian Journal of Economics, No. 1.

Kenen, P. B. (1969), 'The Theory of Optimum Currency Areas: An Eclectic View', in 'Monetary Problems of the International Economy', Mundell, R. and Swoboda, A. (eds.), The University of Chicago Press, Chicago.

Krugman, P. (1992), 'Integration, Specialization, and Regional Growth: Notes on 1992, EMU and Stabilization', Paper presented at the International Conference 'The Transition to Economic and Monetary Union in Europe', Banco de Portugal and CEPR, January.

Machlup, F. et al. (1972), 'International Monetary Problems', American Enterprise Institute, Washington.

Masson, P., Mélitz, J. (1990), 'Fiscal Policy Independence in a European Union', CEPR Discussion Paper No. 516, January.

Mattoon, R., Testa, W. (1992), 'Caution: State and Local Government Brake for Recession', The Federal Reserve Bank of Chicago, March, No. 5.

McDougall, D. (1977), 'The Role of Public Finance in European Economic Integration', Bruxelles, EC Commission.

Mundell, R. A. (1961), 'A Theory of Optimum Currency Areas', American Economic Review, vol. 51, pp. 657–665.

Mussa, M. (1991), 'Monetary and Fiscal Policy in a Unified Europe', Carnegie-Rochester Conference on Public Policy, No. 35, pp. 223–60.

OECD (1989), 'Structural Adjustment in OECD Countries', Paris.

OECD (1986), 'Flexibility in the Labour Market', Paris.

Padoa-Schioppa, T. et al. (1987), 'Efficiency, Stability and Equity: A Strategy for the Evolution of the Economic System of the European Community', Oxford University Press, Oxford.

Poloz, S. S. (1990), 'Real Exchange Rate Adjustment Between Regions in a Common Currency Area', mimeo, February.

Sachs, J., Sala-i-Martin, X. (1991), 'Fiscal Federalism and Optimum Currency Areas: Evidence for Europe from the United States', NBER Working Paper No. 3855, October.

Stockman, A. C. (1987), 'Sectoral and National Aggregate Disturbances to Industrial Output in Seven European Countries', NBER Working Paper No. 2313, July.

Stotsky, J. (1991), 'Coping with State Budget Deficits', Business Review of the Federal Reserve Bank of Philadelphia, January–February.

Tootell, G. (1990), 'Central Bank Flexibility and the Drawbacks to Currency Unification', New England Economic Review, May–June, pp. 3–16.

Van der Ploeg, F. (1990), 'Macroeconomic Policy Coordination During the Various Phases of Economic and Monetary Integration in Europe', European Economy.

Von Hagen., J. (1991), 'Fiscal Arrangements in a Monetary Union – Evidence from the US', Indiana University Discussion Paper No. 58, March.

Weber, A. (1991), 'EMU and Asymmetrics and Adjustment Problems in the EMS – Some Empirical Evidence', in 'The Economics of EMU', European Economy, Special Edition 1.

Wyplosz, C. (1991), 'Monetary Union and Fiscal Policy Discipline', CEPR Discussion Paper No. 488, January.

Notes

1 Analyses of the US as reference optimal currency area have also been carried out by Eichengreen (1990a, b), Bayoumi and Eichengreen (1992), Atkeson and Bayoumi (1991), Sachs and Sala-i-Martin (1991), Poloz (1990), Emerson et al. (1990).

2 These results are consistent with those of Weber (1991), who finds that shocks to inflation rates and other nominal variables are highly symmetrical between EMS countries; besides, the asymmetrical components have been shrinking. Supply shocks have also been fairly symmetrical. Cohen and Wyplosz (1989) found that symmetrical shocks to the French and German economies are much larger than asymmetric shocks.

3 Bayoumi and Eichengreen (1992) distinguish between demand and supply shocks depending on the price and output response to shocks. Their empirical analysis suggests that demand shocks affecting EC countries are smaller than those affecting US regions (with a different regrouping from ours). Supply shocks affecting the EC countries are similar in amplitude to those affecting the US regions. However, their analysis covers a period (1962–1988) of widely changing exchange rates, in which some countries such as Portugal, Greece and Spain were not for the most part members of the EC.

4 For a brief description of the methodology see the Appendix.

5 The average variance of sectoral shares in manufacturing production is 8.4 in the EC, 7.5 in EC10, 7.8 in EC6; in the US it is 18.0, in 1989. Krugman (1992) examines a more broadly aggregated set of regions within the EC and the US and also finds that specialization is much greater in the US.

6 According to Kenen (1969) 'a well diversified national economy will not have to undergo changes in its terms of trade as often as a single product national economy'.

7 Krugman (1992) gives some anecdotal evidence on the geographical distribution of auto production in the EC and the US, showing that in the latter it is more localized. It is interesting to see that from 1980 to 1990 the concentration of automobile production in the EC has strongly decreased. The variance of production shares of the 6 largest producing countries has fallen by about 20 per cent. In 1991 Spain had overtaken Italy to become the third producer in the EC. Furthermore, production has started in Portugal, which in 1991 produced 0.5 per cent of the automobiles manufactured in the EC.

8 On this, see also Bertola (1992).

9 The high degree of real wage rigidity in the EC might in fact explain why recently EC countries have rarely used the exchange rate as an instrument of adjustment.

10 This result is confirmed by Bruno and Sachs (1985) and Coe (1985).

11 Fully aware of the limitations of his simple model, Mundell (1961) explained that: 'if labour and capital are insufficiently mobile within a country, then flexibility of the external price of the national currency cannot be expected to perform the stabilization function attributed to it, and one could expect varying rates of unemployment or inflation in the different regions'. Following this reasoning, Mundell noted that Canada, which does not have substantial labour mobility among its regions, is not a good candidate for flexible exchange rates.

12 De Grauwe and Van Haverbeke (1991) found similar evidence.

13 As Ingram (1973, p.25) pointed out: 'Society may prefer to maintain a certain dispersion of population and to resist tendencies towards its concentration in a few urban areas, even at a cost of reduced output and efficiency. Nations have a variety of regional economic and social programs through which they attempt to deal with problems of regional imbalance. These programs can continue to function in a monetary union, and capital market integration may even increase their effectiveness'.

14 According to Kenen (1969, p. 48) 'when there is immobility between single-product regions of a single nation, it may be very difficult to maintain full employment and price stability throughout its territory; the nation must rely on rather sophisticated internal policies to reallocate demand rather than augment or curb it'.

15 Early proponents of this instrument were Kenen (1969), Ingram (1973) and Allen (1976). For more recent work, see Masson and Mélitz (1990).

16 Military spending, for instance, which amounts to about one fourth of non-interest federal expenditure, is concentrated in a handful of states such as California, Florida, Virginia and Texas.

17 On average, the state and local budgets have recorded a surplus, which in 1991 amounted to $30 billion (0.5 per cent of GDP), $5 billion more than in 1990. The federal budget, by contrast, recorded a deficit of $171 billion (3 per cent of GDP). In certain years, such as 1981, the states' surplus matched the federal deficit. In 1991 the net interest paid by the federal government on its debt amounted to $195 billion, while state and local governments had net interest receipts of $66 billion.

18 See Eichengreen (1990b).

19 Stotsky (1991), Mattoon and Testa (1992).

20 A comparison of the rates of growth of personal and disposable income in the last decade reveals that in six of the twelve US Federal Reserve districts disposable income grew faster than total personal income in fast growing areas or slower than personal income in slow-growing ones. This evidence shows that budgetary policy has in some cases widened the divergence in the growth rates.

21 Article 104c of the Treaty states that a deficit is excessive if it exceeds 3

per cent in relation to gross domestic product, unless:
'• either the ratio has declined substantially and continuously and reached a
level that comes close to the reference value.
• or, alternatively, the excess over the reference value is only exceptional
and temporary and the ratio remains close to the reference value'.
22 In an early debate, Lutz and Triffin noted that budgetary centralization is
not required for monetary union, while Lundberg and Scitovsky took the
opposite view. See Machlup at al. (1972). For a survey of recent debate see
Inman and Rubinfeld (1991).
23 These issues have been addressed in particular by Buiter and Kletzer
(1990), Wyplosz (1991) and Van der Ploeg (1990).
24 Allen (1976).
25 In some states, small poor regions such as Brittany and Northern Ireland,
receive state transfers for as much as 20 per cent of their income.

"Value-Added" Does Not Pollute

SPECIAL MERIT AWARD

Summary

Economic growth entails the increasing consumption of goods and services. Such consumption is often singled out as the underlying cause of environmental degradation. However, goods and services consist of two elements: raw material and energy inputs on the one hand and added-value resulting from human creativity on the other. This essay argues that while the increasing consumption of the former can, and often does, lead to increasing environmental degradation, the consumption of the latter does not.

Therefore, economic growth should be encouraged as far as possible through the increase in added-value alone not through the consumption of ever greater quantities of energy and raw materials.

In an economy growing in such a way the ratio of GNP to the value of raw materials and energy consumed would fall as economic growth occurred. Growth would result entirely from 'doing more with less'.

Measures which could encourage such growth would include taxing the use of raw materials and energy, reducing value-added tax and tax rates on personal income and corporate profitability and introducing better education. The funds generated from the first element could be used to finance the other two.

Charles L. M. Horner has a degree in engineering and a masters degree in manufacturing engineering from Cambridge University and an MBA from INSEAD. He has worked principally in the financial services sector with an emphasis on venture and development capital. Most recently he has been working with a number of companies in Eastern Europe to help them to adjust to the changing economic circumstances of the region. He is also a Fellow of the Royal Geographical Society with a particular interest in environmental conservation.

7

"Value-Added" Does Not Pollute

CHARLES L. M. HORNER

Traditionally the growth in a country's gross national product (GNP) has been used by economic and financial policy makers as the best measure of the success or failure of their policy. However various deficiencies have been recognised in the use of GNP.

First, GNP makes no allowance for the depreciation in a country's capital stock. Statisticians correct for this by estimating what is termed capital consumption and deducting this from GNP to give net national product. In 1989, the UK's GNP was £443 billion and its estimated capital consumption £56 billion, or 12.6% of GNP. This estimate for capital consumption may be compared with the estimate for the UK's total net capital stock in 1989 of £1,458 billion.

The level of capital consumption is therefore not insignificant. However, it is often ignored because it is difficult to estimate and because it is assumed that it remains approximately constant as a proportion of GNP so that GNP growth figures remain unaffected.

The second deficiency is a more recent arrival. It related to the fact that GNP makes no allowance for a wide variety of factors which have an important impact on our quality of life. These factors include pollution, the destruction of forests, traffic congestion and so on.

This second deficiency may in fact be viewed as an extension of the first. The concept of a country's capital stock needs only to be extended to include all those other assets, which have never been purchased and so never appear in traditional national accounts, but which are nevertheless vital elements of human existence. Such assets would include the availability of clean air and fresh water, fertile farm land, forests and so on. This second deficiency would then, once again, become one of failing to make suitable provision for any depreciation in this extended stock of assets.

For the purposes of this essay the term 'environment' is used to describe all those assets which would be newly included in this extended concept of a country's capital stock.

The fact that GNP figures are not adjusted for changes in the state of the environment can be attributed to two reasons. First, there was, until recently, the belief that the environment was inexhaustible so that there was no need to make any adjustment for its depreciation. Second, GNP as a measure is expressed in monetary terms so that a change in the state of the environment would need to be similarly stated if it were to be included. Attributing monetary values to such changes is an extremely difficult and highly subjective task. It has therefore been easiest simply to ignore them.

The belief that the environment is inexhaustible is not completely unfounded. It should be remembered that each year the environment receives its own massive annual 'income' in the form of solar energy. This income is what fuels plant growth and allows the environment to regenerate itself. In the past the environment's regenerative ability has in general easily exceeded the demands man has made upon it so that the issue of depreciation could be genuinely ignored. In addition, for many millions of years, some of this annual income was saved in the form of fossil fuels which now provides us with an enormous inheritance to cushion the impact of depreciation.

Today, however, there can be no doubt that the state of environment is depreciating: the availability of fertile land, of clean water, of forests, of fossil fuels and so on is shrinking continuously.

Furthermore, there is no reason to believe that the growth in the level of this depreciation can be ignored. In general, the monetary value of a country's environment, although impossible to quantify precisely, must be several times higher than the value of its capital stock; the relative importance of the former over the latter in sustaining life itself dictates this difference in value. Even tiny changes to the value of a country's environment would therefore have a significant effect on a country's GNP and could certainly outweigh average annual growth.

It is not satisfactory therefore to assume that changes in the state of the environment should be ignored in calculating a country's economic growth simply because they cannot be accurately quantified in monetary terms. Instead, while accepting the problem of precisely measuring a country's environmentally-adjusted GNP, growth should be encouraged in a way which does not cause further depreciation to the environment. This approach would at least lead to a genuine increase in GNP.

The object of this essay is to examine what changes could be made by economic and financial policy makers to promote such growth.

A key step in addressing this issue is to realise that macro-economic performance represents no more than the sum total of the economic behaviour of individuals. During the past decade or so, the importance of the individual in setting the macro-economic parameters of economies has been increasingly recognised. Hence, for instance, the stress now placed upon the key role played by individual entrepreneurs in generating economic growth.

The driving force behind the economic activity of the individual is the satisfaction of need. To achieve this individuals seek to consume products and services. Indeed we are all most often referred to, by economists, as consumers. However man is capable not only of consuming but also of creating. Indeed, without the ability to create, life would have little meaning. Economists refer to the act of creating as adding value.

The products and services we consume are therefore a combination of natural resources (whether energy or raw material) and of human creativity or added-value. Their relation to the satisfaction of a need may be seen thus:

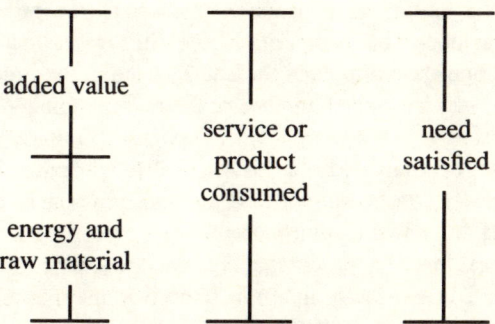

Economic growth will result from greater satisfaction of need. This implies a greater consumption of services and products. This in turn could lead to a greater consumption of added-value or a greater consumption of energy and raw materials, or, normally, to a greater consumption of both. To examine the consequences for the depreciation of the environment of such growth we must therefore examine the effects of the consumption of these two constituent parts.

It is often said that consumption itself is the root cause of environmental depreciation. However, it is the contention of this essay that it is only the consumption of the energy and raw material inputs, rather than of the service or product as a whole, which is damaging.

Added-Value does not Pollute

This contention is best illustrated by two simple examples:

i) Air pollution in Central London results not from the consumption of travel services (whether supplied by a taxi, a bus, a train or a private driver) but from the consumption of fossil fuels that the provision of such travel services entail. That part of the overall service provided by the driver of the vehicle himself is not itself damaging to the environment. After all, if a taxi driver were to become a rickshaw driver he could supply the same service with no adverse impact on the environment.

ii) Once the energy stored in a battery has been consumed the problem of disposing of the battery arises. Disposal is often achieved using land-fill sites but over time the battery can break down allowing poisonous chemicals to leak into the soil, depreciating the environment. However, what causes the problem here is the disposal, not of the battery itself, but of the chemicals, the raw materials used to create it. The creative value added to these raw materials to turn them into a battery disappears harmlessly as the product is consumed and does not itself pollute the site. (Note that in all such examples one should include the energy used in the production of a product or service as just another of the raw materials necessary for its creation.)

The same sort of analysis holds true for all environmental problems provided it really can be shown that the consumption of added-value does not itself degrade the environment.

Strictly speaking, the process of adding value does itself involve consumption. To be creative man must survive and to survive he must consume. *However, man will consume whether or not he exercises his creative abilities.* Therefore, to assess the impact of adding value on the environment one must look solely at the marginal changes in consumption that it creates.

Most people have the potential to be creative and to add value to varying degrees. However, some consumption is involved in the education or training necessary to unlock this potential. Education and training though are highly people-intensive occupations and therefore themselves involve principally the consumption of added-value and not of raw materials or energy.

A greater problem, however, is that a more creative worker will in general earn more and will therefore have the ability to consume more.

However, this is the issue at the heart of all economic growth. Growth feeds growth. It would be unfair therefore to penalise value-added growth alone in this respect.

Furthermore, a macro-economic policy which encouraged adding value rather than the consumption of raw materials and energy should also ensure that new demand thus generated would be similarly satisfied. Indeed the ideal policy would stimulate economic growth entirely through adding ever greater value to a constant or, better still, declining flow of raw materials and energy. If the consumption of raw materials and energy could be held constant then the appropriate charge by which GNP figures should be adjusted to allow for depreciation of the environment, whatever its absolute level, would, arguably, remain constant. One could then be sure that any recorded growth in GNP represented a real increase in economic well-being.

The key indicator in judging the success of such a policy would be the ratio of GNP to the value of raw materials and energy consumed, a 'resource intensity ratio'. Under a poor policy this ratio would remain constant showing that raw material and energy consumption, and therefore the rate of increase in the depreciation of the environment, were increasing in line with GNP. This in turn could mean that recorded increases in GNP were entirely cancelled by increased damage to the environment. However, under a successful policy the ratio would fall as GNP rose.

What this policy amounts to is 'doing more with less'. In its simplest form this would mean no more than reducing the amount of material or energy used to produce a given product. But it could also mean making much greater use of a given product to reduce the demand for replacements or indeed satisfying a perceived need in a quite different, less resource intensive manner. The alternative solutions to the problem of 'doing more with less' would be limited only by man's innate creative abilities and by the incentives or restrictions imposed on him by macro-economic policy.

Three short examples will serve as an illustration:

i) Imagine a country in which half the inhabitants can afford to purchase a new bicycle regularly, while the other half cannot, but in which no mechanism exists for trading in second-hand bicycles. Every few years half the inhabitants buy new bicycles and scrap their old ones since they have no alternative use for them. Meanwhile the poor half possess no means of transport since bicycles are the only way of getting around. Then an entrepreneur sets up a second-hand bicycle shop or publishes a magazine publishing details of old bicycles for sale. Suddenly the poorer inhabitants can afford transport. They have benefited entirely from the value which has been added to the previously useless second-hand bicycles by the creative talents of the entrepreneur. Economic growth has been achieved but without any increase in raw material and energy usage.

ii) Several years later, in the same country, the second-hand bicycles start breaking down but there is no repair shop. Half the inhabitants are again without transport since, having each purchased one second-hand bicycle, they cannot afford another. Luckily however a trained mechanic arrives. He is able to mend the bicycles and all the inhabitants have transport once more. Again needs have been satisfied, and economic growth achieved, without consuming any further raw materials.

iii) Imagine two carpenters, one skilled the other less so. Both are given the same quantity of wood. The skilled one creates a table of great beauty and value which lasts, as the treasured possession of several owners, for a century or more. The less skilled one makes a table which has to be burnt after a few years because it simply falls to pieces. Since his table has lasted for so much longer, the skilled carpenter has clearly satisfied a much greater need than the other by adding much more value to his raw material. The economy in which the skilled carpenter lives will therefore have the lower resource intensity factor.

iv) Consider finally a great artist. With a tiny usage of raw materials, no more than a canvas and some paint, he can create a painting which can satisfy the needs of the viewing public for hundreds of years. A vandal with a spray can however does nothing but degrade the environment. The resource usage is the same in both cases but the added value and satisfaction of need are hugely different.

What tangible policies might therefore be employed to promote a move to economic growth with a rapidly falling resource intensity ratio?

The following are possibilities:

i) Service industries should be encouraged as much as manufacturing industry. The provision of services is in general less raw material and energy intensive than manufacturing and yet, as the second-hand bicycle and repair shop examples above show, a good service industry can satisfy a consumer's need most efficiently.

ii) The use of raw materials and energy should be taxed. Such a tax could be levied at progressively higher rates as usage increases. By contrast taxes on personal income and corporate taxes, both functions of the value added by an individual or a company, and VAT itself should be reduced.

The key issue here is that companies should find it more profitable to maximize human added-value in a product and to minimize the raw materials and energy elements. This is not likely to happen if, as is currently the case, most taxes are levied on the added-value created by individuals and companies.

iii) Although most people have the potential to create and add value, many will require education and training to unlock it. As already noted, education is itself a high value-adding activity and is essential if the supply side of the economy is to be prepared for growth with a falling resource intensity.

Education can also help in another way. Throughout this essay the tacit assumption has been made that consumers present a fixed set of demands which must be satisfied in the least resource intensive manner possible. In fact education may be used to change the needs themselves so that they can be more easily satisfied with a lower consumption of raw materials and energy.

For instance, if a child can be taught to enjoy vegetarian food rather than meat he will grow up satisfying his nutritional needs more effectively since the cultivation of vegetables is a less resource intensive activity than the production of meat.

Again, if a potential vandal can be taught to enjoy music and the theatre he may find it more pleasurable to pass his leisure time benefiting from the creative talents of musicians and actors rather than spending it detracting from the value of the urban environment.

iv) Recycling must be a key priority. When a litter collector picks up an aluminium can from the road side and sends it to be recycled he is adding enormous relative value since the can is immediately transformed from an eyesore into a useful object. Clearly, applying human creativity to the problem of devising better ways of recycling products and materials will provide huge scope for future, low resource intensity growth.

Recycling can be encouraged by ensuring that the use of land-fill sites, representing as it does the consumption of a natural resource, is properly taxed and by exempting recycled materials from the tax on raw materials described above.

v) Finally, the 'hard-nosed' politician should note two things:

First, there is no reason why the measures outlined above should have a net effect on government expenditure. Money raised from taxes on raw materials and energy could be used to reduce income, profit and value added taxes and finance increased training and education.

Second, all these policies are designed to maximise the human added-value in a product or service. In turn this should mean a greater, and more rewarding, use of a country's work-force. These policies could thus help to reduce the high levels of unemployment currently found in many countries.

Ultimately, then, future prosperity will depend on our ability to use our own creative talents to the full. Economic policy makers must therefore seek to stress the role of each one of us not simply as consumer but also as creator, looking to do as much as possible with as little as possible.

An Announced Downward Path for Inflation

SPECIAL MERIT AWARD

Summary

New Zealand's experience with a rather unique variant of monetary policy is described in this essay. Monetary policy in New Zealand is aimed at the achievement of price stability—not in itself unusual internationally, in terms of stated objectives. The uniqueness lies in the unusually well-defined specification of the target.

Important elements of the targeting framework include: price stability is defined in quantitative terms in a formal agreement between the Minister of Finance and the Governor of the Reserve Bank; a time period is specified for the achievement of price stability; the extent of variation allowed in outcomes around the target is prescribed; and a downward path for inflation was publicly announced. This essay explains the reasons for announcing a disinflation path, describes experience with the approach and draws out some early lessons.

The objective of monetary policy is specified in a manner akin to a 'rule'. But the Reserve Bank has been given 'discretion' in monetary policy implementation. The essay argues that this institutional structure is an appropriate mix of 'rules' and 'discretion'. The essay also argues that the framework provides a good basis for the development of policy credibility. Ultimately, credibility is derived from results. The publicly advertised intentions of the monetary authorities in New Zealand give a clear and unambiguous basis for judging results.

Behaviour adjustments are emerging, most significantly within the Reserve Bank itself. But changes have also become evident in the behaviour of financial markets, wage and price setters, and the government.

Peter W. E. Nicholl is Deputy Governor (Policy) and Deputy Chief Executive of the Reserve Bank of New Zealand. He was Chief Economist of the Bank from 1982 to 1985. He was President of the New Zealand Association of Economists in 1983 and 1984. He has a BCA (Honours) degree with first-class honours in economics from Victoria University of Wellington. He has published numerous articles on New Zealand monetary policy and financial markets.

David J. Archer is a Senior Adviser in the Bank's Economic Department, and holds a degree in economics from the Victoria University of Wellington. He is a member of the Bank's Monetary Policy Committee. His career includes a period as an economist in the European Department of the International Monetary Fund.

8

An Announced Downward Path for Inflation

PETER W. E. NICHOLL AND DAVID J. ARCHER

This essay has the objective of informing an international audience of New Zealand's experience with a rather unique variant of monetary policy. Monetary policy in New Zealand is aimed at the achievement of price stability. That in itself is not so unusual, as price stability is the stated objective of the monetary policy of many countries around the world. The uniqueness lies in the specification of the target, which is unusually well defined.

The specification of the target involves a number of elements.

- Price stability as a concept is defined in quantitative terms.
- A time period is specified for the achievement of price stability, which is important because the initial starting position was away from the target.
- The extent of variation allowed in outcomes around the target is prescribed.

Closely intertwined with these unique elements is a publicly announced downward path for inflation. The construct of an announced downward path encapsulates and reflects much of the Reserve Bank of New Zealand's views on the appropriate role for monetary policy, and on the use of monetary policy techniques.

Accordingly, this paper elaborates on the reasons for announcing a disinflation path in New Zealand, and on experience with the approach. There are a number of important early lessons to be derived from experience to date. In order to draw these out, it is important first to understand something of the historical and institutional background, which is a crucial part of the framework within which monetary policy is set in New Zealand.

The next section briefly summarises the recent New Zealand history with regard to monetary policy and inflation performance. Following this, two sections describe the new institutional arrangements for monetary policy that were embedded in new legislation in 1989, and some of the theoretical underpinnings for the new approach. Practical implementation of the new policy framework, and experience with this implementation, are discussed next. Finally, a short section draws out some of the more important policy conclusions.

A Short History

New Zealand experienced double digit inflation for most of the period since the first oil shock. Cumulative inflation (on a CPI basis) between 1974 and 1988 (inclusive) was 480 per cent. A brief, but temporary, fall in inflation to below 5 per cent occurred in the early 1980s, but only as a result of a distortionary wage, price, dividend and interest rate freeze. Throughout the period, monetary policy faced multiple and varying objectives which were seldom clearly specified, and only rarely consistent with achievement of inflation reduction.

As a result of this experience, inflation expectations were deeply entrenched in New Zealand society.

Alongside this poor inflation performance, and ultimately providing the catalyst for change, was an equally dismal growth performance. Over the decade and a half from 1974 to 1988, growth in New Zealand averaged only 1.4 per cent per annum, while public sector and overall external indebtedness rose dramatically.

The New Policy Framework

Since early 1990 the Reserve Bank of New Zealand has been operating under the auspices of a new Act. The Act is fundamentally different from the legislation that preceded it. The key elements of the new legislation are:

• The price stability goal is now entrenched in law. The statute says 'the primary function of the Bank is to formulate and implement monetary policy directed to the economic objective of achieving and maintaining stability in the general level of prices'. The clause in the preceding legislation had multiple objectives—price stability, economic growth, full employment, and balance of payments equilibrium.

- Secondly, the Bank now has effective independence to implement monetary policy in pursuit of its statutory objective, without limitations on the technique except that the choices made must 'have regard to the efficiency and soundness of the financial system'. This means that while the objective of monetary policy is specified in a manner akin to a rule (as will be indicated shortly), the monetary authorities have been given (and use) discretion in monetary policy implementation. No intermediate targets—in the form of monetary aggregates or any other financial variable—are used.

- Ultimately, however, the legislation recognises that any choices on the tradeoffs between monetary policy and other economic policy objectives are the prerogative of the government, and mechanisms are provided in the legislation for these choices to be exercised. In this way, the legislative framework is consistent with a Westminster approach to democracy. The government sets the target, and could change it through legislatively specified procedures. The Reserve Bank cannot change the target that it has been given.

- But, in stark contrast with earlier legislation, the way in which the tradeoff choices must be effected means that all choices on the objectives for monetary policy must be made public and are therefore transparently obvious to the community.

- Along with the operational independence goes accountability for monetary policy implementation decisions. The main mechanism is a requirement to publish a detailed Monetary Policy Statement at least every six months. A Select Committee of Parliament examines the Bank following the publications of each Statement. The main sanction for poor performance in relation to the objective is the explicitly-provided for ability of the Minister of Finance to sack the Governor.

For clarity and accountability, 'stability' and the 'general level of prices' need definition. They are not defined in the legislation, but the Act requires the Governor of the Bank and the Minister of Finance to agree on the definition, and to set this out publicly in a Policy Targets Agreement. The Governor is accountable for the outcome of monetary policy in relation to the quantified inflation targets in the Policy Targets Agreement.

The Policy Targets Agreement defines price stability as 0–2 percent annual increases in the Consumer Price Index. The CPI is used, not because it is any more perfect a measure of changes in the 'general price level' than other indices, but because it is the most widely known and the best understood index. However, the Agreement also requires the Bank to monitor a range of other price indices. The above-zero rate of inflation specified reflects index number problems, the survey methodology, and the difficulty of adjusting for new goods or for improvements in quality. Effectively, a judgement has been made that 1 percent CPI inflation is consistent with stability in the general level of prices.

Provision is made for inflation outcomes outside this 0–2 percent band. Large exogenous supply shocks, such as oil shocks, or direct shocks to the price level arising from indirect tax changes by the government, would force a shift in monetary policy to offset them if there were no caveats that provided for departures from the target. Forcing monetary policy to offset the effects on the price level of such shocks would, it is believed, cause real costs that would be out of all proportion to the benefits of short-run price stability. But it is clearly important that caveats to the price stability target are not so all encompassing, or so loosely defined, as to let domestically sourced inflationary pressures be accommodated.

Because inflation was over 5 percent at the time that the legislation was enacted the Policy Targets Agreement had to specify a time frame for the achievement of price stability. The choice of that time frame represents one of the points at which the government can exercise its ultimate right to determine the tradeoffs between monetary policy and other policy objectives. The initial Policy Targets Agreement signed in March 1990 called for achievement of 0–2 percent inflation by December 1992 and maintenance of price stability thereafter. Partly as a result of a view that the output and employment costs of the speed of adjustment implicit in this time frame were too high, the new government elected in October 1990 deferred the target date by one year.

It should be noted that perpetual deferral of the target date does not provide an easy way out for the Government. The Policy Targets Agreement is a contract between the Government and the Governor of the Bank. The Governor must be satisfied that the Agreement is consistent with the Bank's statutory price stability objective. If s/he is not satisfied, the Government must explicitly and publicly over-ride the price stability objective. A mechanism is provided in the legislation for doing this—again, reflecting the ultimate right of the Government to choose to make a tradeoff. But, in order to do as much as possible to entrench the price stability objective, the Act stipulates that any over-ride of that objective can only last a year. The government must explicitly and publicly renew the over-ride each year.

A Monetary Policy Theoretic Interpretation

In some respects, the policy approach outlined above is thoroughly in tune with the theory, especially in relation to the single-minded focus on price stability. But in other respects, the consistency is not so obvious. There is, as noted, no role for intermediate targets in the New Zealand monetary policy operating method; related to this, nor are there clear 'rules' for the short-term conduct of policy. A considerable amount of discretion is provided to the monetary authorities to juggle the levers of policy as they see fit. Nonetheless, it is fair to claim that New Zealand has a framework that provides a good basis for the development of policy credibility, and as a result, the minimisation of the real interest rate costs of potentially time-inconsistent policy.

An explanation of the theoretical underpinnings of the New Zealand policy approach, and the foregoing claims for it, is available in an article by Robert Flood and Peter Isard in the September 1989 edition of the IMF's Staff Papers. Considering the rules versus discretion debate, Flood and Isard examine the properties of the alternative policies within a world in which the structure of the macro-economy, and the nature of the shocks to the economy, are not well known. They argue that in such a world, the usually-preferred fully state-contingent rules are unworkable for practical reasons. Such rule systems are just too complicated. Simple, or partially state-contingent, rules do not necessarily in these circumstances work better than the alternative of complete discretion. It depends on where the shocks are coming from and the state of knowledge of the policy makers.

In principle, a mix of discretion and a partially state-contingent rule could perform better than either of the alternatives. The trick is to find institutional structures that give strong enough incentives for the policy makers to follow the rule in normal times, but not so strong incentives that major disturbances are not accommodated by way of a temporary departure from the rule.

While Flood and Isard are not addressing exactly the kind of approach adopted in New Zealand, there are some very close parallels. The New Zealand framework has a clear and, as previously noted, uniquely well defined rule for the inflation target. Discretion is allowed for in two areas: in the choice of policy technique, and in respect of the target itself.

As to technique, the incentive structures are such that the choices made must be consistent with the policy objective. The Bank, and particularly the Governor, is fully accountable for the outcome. The Governor may be sacked for missing the target.

As for the target itself, the transparency of any departure from the objective of price stability, or from the particular quantitative definition of price stability, provides a strong check on attempts to achieve short term output goals at the expense of the longer term objective. It is not possible for the Governor to take 'under the table' instructions to generate a surprise inflation without exposing himself to the risk of dismissal if the formal inflation targets are not subsequently achieved. Any substantive modification of the price stability objective must be done in writing, and in public.

So the New Zealand approach fits very well with Flood and Isard's general characterisation of optimal monetary policy arrangements in an uncertain world.

Note also that the usual criticisms of an inflation target involve the performance of the policy in the face of supply shocks. Amongst the most common supply shocks in New Zealand are changes in the terms of trade. The framework makes explicit allowance for such shocks.

Applying the Framework

It was quite clear from the outset that the mere enactment of the legislation would not be enough to establish monetary policy credibility, especially when the poor history of monetary policy in New Zealand is taken into account. There did not seem to be a large 'announcement effect' on the passing of the legislation. Ultimately, credibility is derived from results—and particularly from results in relation to publicly advertised intentions. A thousands reiterations of the Reserve Bank's adherence to the objective would mean little compared with the doubts that would arise if inflation did not track in a manner consistent with getting to the target.

For this reason, early on the Bank set out a series of indicative inflation ranges that it believed would be consistent with arrival at the target by due date, and maintenance of the target thereafter. These ranges were 2.5–4.5 per cent for the year to December 1991 and 1.5–3.5 per cent for the year to December 1992. These inflation ranges have indeed proved to be very important to the policy process, although their role has altered over the time since they were put in place.

Over the years, much has been made in the monetary policy literature of the potential role for *intermediate* policy targets. Such targets include monetary aggregates, including base money; the nominal exchange rate; and less often, money incomes.

The key requirement of intermediate targets is that they provide most useful information on the likely achievement of the inflation target than the inflation target by itself. In principle, each of the candidates has the advantage of providing more timely information than the inflation result. In practice, that is not so clear. Empirically, in New Zealand most monetary aggregates are not leading indicators of inflation. Nor indeed is it empirically obvious that information on the path of money incomes comes any earlier than information on inflation outcomes, even though the dynamic response of an economy to a money surprise usually involves an adjustment of output before the bulk of the corresponding price effects emerge. The technical problems of measuring the relevant variables are part of the answer to this apparent inconsistency.

More fundamentally, though, the short term instability of the behavioural relationships involved is fatal to the idea that the intermediate monetary aggregate targets would perform the intended role well. And as to the exchange rate as an intermediate target, the context of a small open economy with relatively concentrated trade patterns gives rise to a range of other problems associated with impending desirable real exchange rate adjustment in response to certain shocks.

Given these difficulties, it seemed that the better option was to indicate the inflation track that was expected to be consistent with achievement of the objective, and allow relatively free reign to the Bank's technical judgements on the nature and evolution of the relevant behavioural relationships. However, economic agents apparently did not rapidly adopt the indicative inflation ranges as a central piece of information in their analyses of the likely future path of monetary policy. Frequent demands arose for a detailed specification of the Bank's policy reaction function, with much focus on the question of what interest rate and exchange rate outcomes the Bank believed consistent with the desired policy stance.

In part, this may have simply been due to lack of experience with the indicative inflation ranges. While there were occasions when policy was tightened in response to the Bank's publicly stated concerns that inflation was threatening to break out of the top of the indicative ranges, until some time later there were no occasions when policy reacted to a threatened undershoot of the range. That situation did arise in September 1991 when policy was explicitly eased. This event reinforced the message that the Bank was moving to harden the ranges into more explicit 'en route' or 'way point' targets than had originally been envisaged.

With these changes, the attention of financial markets and media commentators has come to focus more and more on forecasts of inflation vis-a-vis the inflation targets as the basis for predicting likely monetary policy reactions.

In adopting 'way points' targets for inflation, a number of rather difficult policy choices have to be made. While these choices are also in part relevant for an 'indicative' announced downward path, they become more crucial when hard-ended target ranges are involved. Specifically:

1. First, the shape of the target path needs to be considered. The key questions here relate

- to the economic background that is likely to be encountered over the relevant period—an economy moving out of recession will obviously involve a different inflation path than an economy moving in the other direction;

- to any non-linearities in the ease of reducing inflation—if the costs of inflation-reduction rise as inflation approaches zero, making rapid progress early in the piece will be important; and

- to the desire to obtain credibility—it is important not to be over ambitious in the first phase, as missing the early targets would make the rest of the process much more difficult.

2. Secondly, the width of the 'way point' target ranges have to be established. Too narrow a target range will cause more 'misses', and throw into doubt the technical abilities of the policy makers. Too narrow a range could also set up the prospect of the stance of monetary policy swinging violently in one direction and then the other as various new pieces of information are reacted to. On the other hand, too wide a range would provide little guide to markets

as to the actual policy reaction function, if for no other reason than there would be fewer occasions when the edges of the ranges prompted policy actions.

In the New Zealand case, consideration of the design features of hard inflation target ranges took place in the context of indicative inflation ranges having already been announced, somewhat pre-empting alternative choices. In the event, the announced ranges were not inconsistent with the balance of the Bank's judgement on the above considerations.

How Has It Worked Out In Practice?

It is all very well to claim that we have in New Zealand a well-designed monetary policy approach, but how has it worked out in practice? In particular, what have been the responses to the announced downward path?

As already noted, the early indicative character of the announced inflation ranges might have provided too loose a guide to the community of the likely evolution of policy in the early stages. But behaviour has gradually adapted.

Some evidence in support of this is available in the reaction of the trade union movement to policy over the last couple of years. After watching policy tighten when the Bank became concerned that inflation was not tracking down as desired, the head of the union movement wrote an article that said (and we paraphrase here): 'I don't like what they are doing but we have to plan on the basis that they will be doing it'. There is considerable evidence that the union movement entered the last round of wage negotiations with a completely different inflation outlook than previously. That was illustrated in 1990 in a short-lived 'growth agreement' between the unions and the then government, in which the unions stated a willingness to accept 2 percent wage increases (plus any productivity adjustments) when recorded inflation was still over 5 percent. The agreement itself was short-lived but the low wage rises were nevertheless secured.

Financial markets have for some time been reflecting expectations of falling rates of inflation, consistent with the target path. Interest rates fell by between as much as 7 percentage points over the 2 years to May 1992, more often than not with financial markets leading and the Reserve Bank accommodating. Following the explicit easing of policy on 25 September 1991 in response to a threatened undershoot of the indicative inflation ranges, there is now a greater understanding of the way-point target nature of the inflation ranges. Quite frequently now, the commentaries of brokers and analysts compare their inflation forecasts vis-a-vis the way-point targets with the Reserve Bank's forecasts vis-a-vis the ranges. From such comparisons, analysts can make informed judgements as to the likely nature of monetary policy settings over the quarters ahead.

But by far the most significant and important behavioural change has taken place inside the policy making machine. The announced downward path for inflation has provided a structure for internal discussions and debates within the Reserve Bank about the appropriate stance of policy. It has also provided the impetus for a number of politically sensitive decisions, notably the tightening of policy in May and August 1990 (in the run-up to the 1990 New Zealand election), a reluctance to accelerate the market-led loosening in monetary conditions through 1991, and the willingness explicitly to ease policy in September 1991. In each case the critical deciding factor behind the tightenings, and the more recent eventual acceleration of the loosening trend, was the outlook for inflation relative to the way-point target ranges over the 1–2 years ahead.

Policy Conclusions

Overall, the use of an announced downward path for inflation has been a very important aspect of the monetary policy strategy in New Zealand.

In particular, setting out a series of way-point targets has given the central bank a clear framework for policy decisions, and has provided the motivation to take policy actions that might be politically difficult.

As a corollary, setting out a path in this way provides tight, and publicly obvious, limits to the central bank's room to take other economic objectives into account, thus reinforcing the single focus of monetary policy on price stability. That is not to say that the Reserve Bank ignores what is happening to output and employment. Rather, such economic developments are incorporated into the analysis precisely because they have a bearing on likely inflation outcomes.

Finally, announced target paths are particularly important given the absence of usable intermediate targets. By providing an alternative to the use of intermediate targets, an announced downward path provides scope for central bank discretion in reacting to perceived shifts in the unstable short term relationships without opening the policy to severe time-inconsistency problems.

Postscript

Since this article was written (October 1991), increasing evidence has become available to attest to the credibility-enhancing effects of the monetary policy framework in New Zealand. Short term interest rates (90 day bank bill rates), which were around 8.1 per cent through most of October 1991, had fallen to 6.1 per cent by mid-September 1992. Five year Government bonds have also fallen, from around 8.7 per cent to 7.1 per cent. These interest rate reductions have exceeded those in New Zealand's international trading partners, both in nominal and in real terms (the latter calculated with either forward or backward looking inflation). The implicit risk premium on New Zealand dollar assets (calculated from real long-term interest rate differentials) has now reduced from an average of 3½ per cent in 1989 to an average of 1½ per cent in the first three-quarters of 1992, despite New Zealand's ongoing exposure to difficult world trading conditions and continued (though slowed) accumulation of external debt.

More direct evidence on the relatively rapid acquisition of monetary policy credibility is also available in a variety of inflation expectation surveys. One, a reasonably wide-ranging survey of business and financial market professionals, shows year-ahead inflation expectation of 2 per cent. A second, covering leading economists only but looking seven years ahead, has inflation staying at 2 per cent throughout. In contrast, New Zealand's inflation rate averaged 12 per cent in the 1970s, and 11.4 per cent in the 1980s. Finally, to indicate that these results are not the product of perpetual stagnation, New Zealand's real growth rate in the years to March 1993 and March 1994 are projected to average 3 per cent.

The Informal Economy: A Vehicle for Growth in Sub-Saharan Africa

SPECIAL MERIT AWARD

Summary

In stark contrast to the mainstream economies of Sub-Saharan Africa, the informal economy continues to thrive, accounting for over 60% of the urban labour force and 20% of GDP in the region. This essay examines that dynamic sector which operates with a quasi-legal status at the fringes of the modern urban economy and has recently begun to gain recognition as a potential engine for economic development.

The growth of the sector is attributed partly to the difficulties of compliance with bureaucratic controls and more recently, to the severe recession afflicting the region which has reduced the employment capacity of the formal sector. The increasing domination by the informal sector in many aspects of industry is traced to the sector's lower prices and greater flexibility. The sector has been active in building up domestic markets and its strong points are identified as cheap job creation, good returns on investment and local raw material utilisation as well as the crowning glory of its being the only buffer against the region's rapidly growing labour force.

The failure of large-scale industrialisation efforts in the region is blamed on the inability to finance such ambitious plans, and the bustling small scale enterprises of the informal sector, requiring as they do little external financial help, are postulated as a more viable alternative.

Some major problems of the sector, to wit, low productivity, inadequacy of capital, poor skills and generally hostile official attitudes, are identified and possible solutions proffered. In the light of the failure of transplanted policies for economic recovery, the essay concludes by suggesting a serious evaluation of the informal economy with a view to formulating the dynamics thereof as a launch-pad for an indigenous model of development in the sub-continent.

Peter C. Ntephe is a solicitor and partner in the Port Harcourt (Nigeria) law firm of Ntephe, Smith & Wills. He was formerly Head of Corporate Law Division, Serena David Dokubo & Company. He has written a number of published papers on foreign investment and related economic issues. He is currently completing his postgraduate thesis on 'The Legal Framework for Managing Corporate Insolvencies in Nigeria'.

9

The Informal Economy: A Vehicle for Growth in Sub-Saharan Africa

PETER C. NTEPHE

It is 7:30 a.m. in the West African town and Ugo Okafor has been at his sewing machine in the little room in front of his house for close to an hour. He will not retire until well past 9:00 p.m. by which time his 'Ugo-Best Tailoring Industry' (comprising Ugo and two apprentices), may have raked in the local currency equivalent of US$15. Across the road, Apiafi is charging the equivalent of US$2 per vehicle to wash cars at the stream by the highway. In a good day Apiafi washes as many as 10 cars or more.

Ugo and Apiafi are micro-entrepreneurs and in an economic regime in which an executive in a big manufacturing firm or a top civil servant may earn only US$10 a day, they (and millions of others like them) represent the informal economy, the emergent face of capitalism in Sub-Saharan Africa. Covering a wide variety of enterprises from the lowly load-carriers and petty traders to the small but relatively organised business units which employ several people, the informal economy operates at the fringes of the modern urban economy all over Sub-Saharan Africa, and, by International Labour Organisation estimates, accounts for as much as 60 per cent of the urban labour force in the region. For so long viewed by the governments of Africa as an impediment to development, the sector has recently begun to gain recognition as a dynamic vehicle for economic growth and several countries, retreating from abortive attempts at large-scale industrialisation, have started programmes to harness the potential of small and micro scale enterprises.

Across the region in the nether world of food hawkers, shoe makers, mobile barbers, watch repairers et al, the operatives of the sector maintain a quasi-legal status that displays the distinguishing characteristic of a disregard for the licenses, wage structures, income taxes and the numerous other administrative controls inherent in the mainstream economy. From their homes, shanty stalls, push carts and rickety tables set by the highway, the informal entrepreneurs, more often than not, while waging a running battle with government authorities over one permit or another, carry on a bustling trade that by some estimates contributes over 20 per cent of the Gross Domestic Product in the region and as much as 45 per cent in some of the countries.

The problems attendant to compliance with the stifling bureaucratic conditions for establishing business in the formal sector had for long established the informal sector as a significant, if largely unrecorded, factor in Sub-Saharan economies. The more visible reason however for the rapid expansion of the informal economy in recent times is the severe debt-induced recession afflicting the region under which the formal sector has been unable to absorb the substantial increases in the labour force and the more ingenious among the unemployed have been constrained to seek jobs (mostly by self-employment) in the informal sector. It is on this point that the question arises as to whether the sector constitutes a catalyst for capitalism or is merely a stop-gap for unemployment.

While it is possible to view the expansion as strictly a result of the lack of employment in the mainstream economy, (in which case, in a limited market, expansion will soon cease), there is strength in the argument that growth is also a natural response to increased demand for the productivity of the sector. Evidence on the ground supports the view that the informal market contributes much more than just a residual function in Sub-Saharan economies. With widespread devaluation of currencies in the region and the sharp decline of consumer purchasing power in the last decade, the majority of the populace can hardly afford to pay the prices for goods and services emanating from the organised sector. It is little wonder then that the informal entrepreneurs, with their much lower prices and greater flexibility of service have become dominant in many aspects of industry. In most of the region for instance, vehicle maintenance, construction of dwelling houses and retail distribution of consumables are but a few of the areas in which the informal economy holds sway. Increasingly the trend is for the formal sector to source many of its requirements from the informal economy and it is not unusual in Kenya as in Nigeria for the big multinational company to contract out to roadside carpenters, the making of furniture for its superstructure office complex and residences for its executives. As a measure of its growing importance and acceptance, the sector has in official terminology in many of the countries been dubbed 'the parallel market', an improvement on the derisive acronyms of the past.

It may be true, as is often contended, that ultimately only the output from a technologically advanced mainstream economy will make lasting impressions on overseas markets. However, the immediate advantages of the informal sector lie not in its export potentials (which should eventually develop) but in its building up of the domestic markets. Job creation in the sector is cheap, involving as little as a tenth of what would be required in the formal economy and as has been repeatedly displayed by numerous enterprises begun on little more than tact and innate understanding of market forces, returns on investments are relatively high. The conservation of foreign exchange by businesses in the informal economy is also a strong point. With the little capital at the disposal of the entrepreneurs, local raw material utilisation is imperative and the ability of the sector to recycle materials is near legendary. A vehicle fender fabricated from scrap by the itinerant automobile mechanic in Ghana or Cameroon would typically cost only a fifth (or less) of the price of the spare part imported from Europe. Again, unlike the organised private sector, the informal economy has shown little tendency towards capital flight and income accruing is used for sustenance, ploughed back directly into the business or otherwise redistributed within the system. Of course, the crowning glory of the sector has been its ability to buffer the explosion of Sub-Saharan Africa's labour force which the mainstream economy has proved so pitifully incapable of dealing with. The labour force is expected to double in the next quarter of a century and thus far only the informal sector has shown the capacity to create jobs at sufficient rates to absorb the increases.

For decades, governments in the region have pursued large scale industrialisation as the panacea for underdevelopment. With the low per capita incomes prevalent in the region, private enterprise has always been unable to sustain the ambitious levels of industrialisation and the state has had to maintain a near monopoly in the funding of industry. Such a monopoly did not engender competition and coupled with the dubious socio-political considerations and corruption so endemic to public sector projects in Africa, has seen many much-heralded development plans come to nought. With the reversal of state funding of industry and decreasing foreign investment in the continent, it is perhaps only the informal sector, requiring as it does only minute financial assistance from without, that holds any appreciable promise for growth in the immediate future.

Unsurprisingly, the governments of the region, desperate for a solution to the colossal economic problems facing them, are awakening albeit reluctantly to the benefits of encouraging the sector instead of treating it at best with levity and more usually with the subjugation that has typified the past. While the sector is yet to be viewed universally as an integral part of the overall economy, strategies are now being pursued in many countries in conjunction with international aid organisations to support small and micro scale enterprises. A major impediment to the success of such programmes so far has been the lack of consensus among planners as to approach. What is undisputed in any event is that the successes of the sector have been largely self-generated and the role of the state must be restricted merely to the creation of a conducive environment for the informal enterprises to thrive. Any attempt to foist on government the role of producer of goods and assignor of resources, as has been the case in the formal economy, would not only be foolhardy but would rob the informal sector of the spontaneity which has been so instrumental to its growth.

To facilitate small and micro scale enterprise, the acquisition and enhancement of skills by larger segments of the populace must be urgently addressed. The colonially established African education system with its emphasis on literary subjects is ill-suited to the manpower needs of the region and must be overhauled to provide more practical training in technical skills. Aside from formal education, cottage industries where skills are acquired on the job need to be proliferated to train potential entrepreneurs who may thereafter provide, typically from their homes or 'sheds', services in which they have become skilled. Apprenticeships should also be promoted as a cheap but effective way of providing training for self enterprise.

Low productivity has always been identified as a major drawback of small businesses. A three-member family laundry for example can wash, dry and press only so many clothes in any one day. The rapidly increasing number of entrants in the informal market makes it vital that its productivity must be increased to avoid a depreciation of individual incomes. Small scale producers would be availed the economies of scale by forming co-operatives and producer associations which would reduce costs through wholesale purchase of materials and enhance their marketing power. The entrepreneurs also require to be enlightened on the benefits of employing modern, low-cost equipment (as opposed to manual labour or primitive implements) for many of the services they provide. Farm produce has been dramatically increased in many parts of Africa by the simple device of introducing farmers to improved farming implements and cheap fertilizers.

The relative poverty of the Sub-Saharan peoples is another impediment to increased economic activity. Recognising this, some countries have set up funds to provide subsidised credit to small and micro enterprises but fairly stringent collateral requirements have restricted the benefits of those facilities to the upper echelons of the target sector. Such credit should be viewed in part as a social service in which far-reaching concessions must be given so that while the terms should be clear and strictly adhered to, the qualifying conditions would be liberal. Business advisory services can conveniently (and should) be combined with the administration of credit. Furthermore, if producer associations are properly set up, credit can be administered and monitored effectively through the primary societies. It might be possible also for the associations to mobilise the savings which are so lacking in African communities but which could provide the much needed capital to fuel economic activity.

Whatever the incentive(s) adopted to encourage the growth of the informal economy, it remains fact that success would be limited unless the governments of the region make a conscious and complete break from the generally hostile treatment meted to the sector. The unnecessary legislative and administrative restrictions which stunt informal enterprises must be removed and the undue harassment of the sector by public authorities actively discouraged (even by punitive methods, if necessary). It is perhaps only in an economic climate devoid of official disapproval of the informal sector that those resourceful enterprises founded on real demand for their output and nurtured on fierce competition would achieve their true potential.

There is no gain saying the fact that the overall economic performance of Sub-Saharan Africa is steadily deteriorating. The prescriptions formulated by foreign technocrats for reversing the decline of the economies, though impressive in theory, do not appear to have taken into consideration the peculiar financial, socio-political and physical environment of the region and the expected results are nowhere near being realised. In the face of mounting debts, increasing foreign disinvestment in the continent and populations which are growing swiftly beyond manageable proportions, it is not surprising that all economic forecasts for the region remain bleak. The continuing vibrancy of the informal economy in the face of the dire conditions has lent credence to the belief that the answer to revitalising Sub-Saharan economies might lie to a greater extent than is currently accepted in harnessing the vast entrepreneurial energies of the sector and formulating the same as a foundation for an indigenous model of development in the subcontinent. In stark contrast to the stagnation of the mainstream economies, the informal sector, without assistance from the almighty machinery of state, has performed so creditably that economists and policy makers cannot but henceforth seriously evaluate the dynamics of the small scale enterprises and evolve realistic development plans for the region predicated upon the grassroots model of capitalism epitomised by the sector. With its economic quagmire deepening by the day, Sub-Saharan Africa is fast running out of alternatives and it would certainly be a fundamental error if the drive, the dynamism and the promise exhibited by the informal economy are not exploited to the fullest advantage.

References

Higgins, B. 'Economic Development', (*Allahabad: Central Book Depot, 1981*)

Olaloku, F. A. 'Structure of the Nigerian Economy', (*Lagos: Macmillan, 1979*)

Taylor, M. (ed) 'Taxation for African Economic Development'. (*London: Hutchinson, 1970*).

Westlake, M. 'Africa's Last Chance' *South*, No 110, December 1989, pp. 10–11.

Westlake, M. 'Dynamism in the Shadows', *South*, No 112, February 1990, p. 19.

Westlake, M. 'Out of the Shadows', *South*, No 115, May 1990, pp. 12–17.

Unfinished Business of the Single Market Programme

SPECIAL MERIT AWARD

Summary

This essay shows that an important part of the European Community's Single Market Programme, due to be completed by 31st December 1992, remains unfinished. According to the Cecchini Report, about one third of all the economic benefits arising from the Programme were expected to come from the liberalisation of financial services. A significant part of the financial services sector is that which manages life assurance, pensions and investment funds, which together may be described as the long term retail savings management industry. Although there are no longer regulatory barriers to intra-Community trade in much of this industry, the possibility of trade is limited by differences between member states in the tax treatment of long term household savings. While the Community has acted to approximate differences in indirect taxation, so that these are no longer a significant hindrance to trade between member states, the taxation of retail savings and the income arising therefrom falls under the heading of direct taxation, about which there has hitherto been no political agreement. So long as fiscal discrimination persists, there will be no possibility of cross-border trade, and the benefits of the Single Market Programme will not be extended to the long term savings of the Community's households.

David R. F. Simpson is Economist at The Standard Life Assurance Company. He was formerly Professor of Economics at the University of Strathclyde, and Director of the Fraser of Allander Institute; Associate Statistician at the United Nations; and Instructor in Economics at Harvard University. He has published a number of books and articles on a range of economic topics, in particular input–output analysis, political economy and economic growth.

10

Unfinished Business of the Single Market Programme

DAVID R. F. SIMPSON

Introduction

It is well known that by 31 December 1992 it is intended that all the European legislation should be in place to complete the single market amongst the twelve member states of the Community. It is sometimes forgotten that when the Single Market Programme was launched in 1985 freedom of trade was already a reality for most industries within the Community. Tariffs and quotas on intra-Community trade had largely been removed by 1968. The main tasks then remaining to achieve economic union were the lifting of some non-tariff barriers to the free movement of goods and services in a number of industries, together with the removal of regulatory restrictions on the free movement of labour and of capital.

The most prominent amongst those industries whose trade was still restricted in 1985 was financial services—especially retail financial services. While wholesale and corporate banking services and the insurance of large risks by general (i.e. non-life) insurers were traded freely not only throughout Europe but also worldwide, retail banking, fund management, securities dealing and life insurance services, as well as the insurance of non-life mass risks, were confined within the individual domestic markets of the member states.

The importance of the financial services sector in the EC can be illustrated by the fact that the value added by the credit and insurance sectors alone accounted for some 6.5% of the Community's GDP in 1945. In the eight larger Community countries studied by Cecchini[1] insurance premiums amounted to 5% of GDP.

Given the compartmentalisation of the financial services sector and its size, it was not surprising that when Cecchini estimated the value of the economic benefits to be obtained from completion of the Single Market Programme the liberalisation of trade in financial services played a central role. Cecchini estimated that the Single Market Programme as a whole could add by the end of its sixth year as much as 4.5% to the Community's GDP. Of this, no less than 1.5% of the GDP was estimated to be contributed by the liberalisation of financial services alone. Thus, although financial services account for only about one twentieth of Community GDP, the sector was expected to contribute one third of the economic benefits arising from the programme. Furthermore, the liberalisation of the financial services sector would, it was estimated, improve public finances by an amount equal to around 1% of GDP, mainly through a reduction in the debt burden, while its deflationary impact on price levels should be around 1.4%. At the same time it would contribute an additional 440,000 new jobs.[2]

The Nature and Importance of Life Assurance

The life assurance industry has evolved from its beginnings in 16th century Europe from being a supplier of protection against the risk of premature death to being a manager of an individual's investment risk. In most European states today, as in Japan and the USA, the overwhelming proportion of life assurance contracts are savings contracts which contain only a small element of death-risk protection, or none at all. The life assurance premium is therefore no longer a payment for the provision of a risk-bearing service; it is rather a transaction in which a transfer of some of the policyholder's savings to the company is combined with a fee for investment management (and perhaps some risk management) services to be rendered over the period specified in the contract. The joint nature of this transaction has important implications for taxation, as we shall see below. Life assurance companies can therefore appropriately be classified with pension fund and other investment fund managers as providers of long-term retail savings contracts. Although it is impossible to make an accurate estimate, it seems likely that this business may account for perhaps one fifth of the value added by the financial services sector in Europe as a whole.

It is this savings management role which accounts for the importance of the life assurance industry in the contemporary advanced economy. This importance is likely to grow in the next several decades as more and more European citizens acquire greater means of providing for their future consumption needs, and as these needs become ever more pressing as a result of increasing longevity and the rising costs of medical care. A recent estimate[3] has suggested that there may at present be some ECU 700 billion of assets in the balance sheets of pension funds within the European Community, and a further ECU 850 billion or so in those of life assurance companies.

The Removal of Regulatory Barriers

Full attainment of a European single market in financial services implies not simply that financial institutions enjoy complete freedom of establishment and the freedom to provide cross-border services, but also that consumers are free to open accounts, purchase securities and take out insurance policies or bank loans in any member state, and that money and capital are able to circulate freely across intra-Community frontiers.

When the Single Market Programme was launched in 1985 the retail savings industry was tightly enclosed within each state's own markets. This compartmentalisation was maintained by two administrative systems, (i) the regulatory system, and (ii) the tax system, as well as by exchange controls.

In most member states, the supply of retail savings management services was only permitted to those companies which were authorised to conduct business by the regulatory authorities of the state. Authorization was normally granted only if the supplying company established a branch or subsidiary in the state concerned and conformed to detailed and, in many instances, restrictive local regulations concerning the market in which they conducted their business.

In the rare cases where cross-border trade was not explicitly prohibited by statute, it was ruled out by discriminatory taxation provisions. For example, in the United Kingdom, the benefits of long-term savings contracts issued to UK residents by non-resident insurance companies are more heavily taxed than the benefits of similar policies issued by UK insurance companies. Similar provisions of a discriminatory character are to be found in the taxation codes of most member states of the Community.

The regulatory barriers to cross-border trade in investment funds were the first to be lifted. In October 1989, a Directive providing for a 'single passport' for certain types of investment funds was adopted.

This meant that the services of an investment fund authorised by the regulatory authorities of one member state could be sold in all other member states, local regulations notwithstanding.

Cross-border membership of pension funds will not be realised in legislation by the deadline of 31 December 1992. The Commission, however, has declared its intention eventually to legislate to establish this particular freedom, despite the administrative and political difficulties created by the interdependence of social security-based and occupational pension schemes in most member states.

In life assurance, the Third Life Assurance Directive restores the freedom of cross-border trade in life insurance services throughout Western Europe for the first time since 1914. This Directive is expected to be adopted by December 31st 1992 and should come into force in most member states by July 31st 1994. In anticipation of what they believe will be the norms of this forthcoming liberalisation, France, Spain and Italy have all amended their life assurance regulations. Thus the process of competitive deregulation has already begun. Unfortunately, the provisions of the Third Life Directive have been rendered null and void by the continuing existence of fiscal frontiers which show no signs of being removed.

The Significance of Taxation in the Single Market Programme

In the 1985 White Paper which listed the measures judged to be necessary to complete the internal market, one of the three major chapters was devoted to taxation. Significantly, however, the measures envisaged in this chapter related solely to the approximation of indirect taxation, (i.e. the taxation of goods and services), such as VAT and excise duties. These measures are regarded as 'essential' by the Commission whereas harmonisation of direct taxation (i.e. taxation of the incomes of companies, individuals, and savings) is regarded as only 'important'.

Although the Commission argue that indirect tax differences divert trade and distort competition it is difficult to escape the conclusion that the priority given to reducing indirect tax barriers over direct tax barriers is due to the political visibility of the former. Direct tax barriers, however, although politically invisible, may be more impermeable.

As long as appreciable differences in VAT and excise duty rates persisted between member states, then governments felt justified in carrying out frontier checks to ensure that the tax revenue to which they were entitled accrued to them. The abolition of such frontier checks was seen as a key element in the move to complete the internal market. Cecchini, however, found that the elimination of frontier checks would add only 0.4% to Community GDP, i.e. the economic value of the benefit was about one quarter of the benefit to be obtained from the liberalisation of financial services.

While the Commission has succeeded in its attempt to achieve an approximation of VAT and excise duty rates between countries, so that all frontier checks on trade between member states should be abolished on 1 January 1993, it has failed to achieve a similar harmonisation of direct taxes. The Commission's proposals for the introduction of a common system of withholding tax (including a minimum rate of 15%) on interest paid to residents and nonresidents of the EC have failed to secure political agreement amongst the representatives of the Member States.

Thus, the tax position at the beginning of 1992 was that harmonisation of indirect taxes was to be achieved by 1 January 1993. Differences in direct taxation were believed to be of minor importance: finding solutions to such distortions as might arise from this source was left to a committee (the Ruding Committee).[4] This Committee has, however, focused exclusively on the taxation of business savings (profits) and has ignored the taxation of household savings.

However, it remains the case that large parts of the financial services industry, notably life assurance, pensions and investment funds, are characterised by tax systems in most member states which explicitly discriminate against imports. Although Articles 95–98 of the Treaty of Rome prohibit discrimination in the tax treatment of similar domestic and imported commodities, these Articles are concerned simply with the taxation of commodities. They do not cover direct taxes. The taxation of payments to, and benefits from, life insurance companies, pension funds and investment funds is classified as direct taxation. Discriminatory tax treatment of savings is clearly a restriction on the free movement of capital. But because of the joint nature of the transaction, the tax on the savings element is at the same time an indirect tax on the service element of the transaction, and therefore distorts cross-border trade in the same way that the taxation of other commodities does.

Removal of Tax Barriers

Although widely recognised to exist, explicit tax barriers to cross-border trade in life assurance and other retail saving services were, until quite recently, thought likely to be short-lived, since they appeared to violate Articles 48 and 59 of the Treaty of Rome. However, a test case with the support of the Commission was brought before the European Court of Justice by a Mr Bachmann, a German national living in Belgium. Mr Bachmann claimed that a Belgian law providing that life assurance premiums paid in Belgium to an insurance company could only be deducted for income tax purposes if that company was Belgian infringed the relevant articles of the Treaty.

In February 1992 the European Court agreed that the Belgian law did indeed constitute a restriction upon the freedoms provided under Articles 48 and 59, but it ruled that this restriction was justified for tax reasons. If the Belgian tax authorities allowed deduction of premiums for tax purposes, they must also be allowed to recover the tax on the proceeds. This principle appeared to be what the Court had in mind when it referred to the 'coherence' of a tax regime, although that term was nowhere defined in its judgement.

Had the opposite conclusion been reached by the Court, the right of an individual to buy insurance from a company situated in any member state, without being penalised in so doing by the tax laws of his country of residence, would have been upheld. Such a decision would have had strongly positive repercussions for other savings contracts where discriminatory tax treatment exists. So far, the Commission has brought forward no proposals to deal with taxation problems affecting pension funds and investment funds.

What then should be done?

In principle, the substantial differences in taxation that exist between member states need create no obstacle to freedom of trade in savings contracts provided that each member state takes steps to apply the same tax treatment to all contracts effected by residents, whether with domestic or with foreign suppliers. It therefore would be appropriate for the Commission to issue a Directive to the effect that the tax deductibility of premiums and the taxation of proceeds should be applied according to the rules of the member state in which the policyholder is resident, and that there should be no discrimination between sources of supply.

The Commission may be inhibited in introducing such an evidently desirable provision by an amendment introduced to the Rome Treaty at Maastricht, presumably at the behest of national tax authorities, which appears to authorise fiscal discrimination.[5]

It seems that the tax authorities in the individual member states fear a potential loss of tax revenues if residents place their insurances with foreign companies which need not charge and account for taxes to the policyholder's government. Within closed markets each national tax authority could easily keep a check on life and pensions contracts, since all were effected with companies located within their jurisdiction. Once free trade is permitted, control becomes impossible, and accurate tax returns depend on the honesty of the individual policyholder.

In fact, the potential tax revenue losses feared by the authorities may be quite small, since most member states already offer tax relief to most forms of long-term retail savings contracts. Any tax revenue gains from fiscal discrimination are most likely to be outweighed by the welfare losses experienced by consumers denied the opportunity of buying better-performing contracts.

What the tax authorities seem to overlook is that theirs is an objection to *all* forms of capital movement—not just to free trade in life assurance, pensions or investment fund contracts. There are no grounds for singling out retail savings contracts for special treatment. If the principle of allowing the tax authorities to discriminate wherever they fear a potential loss of revenue is upheld, it could be used to justify restrictions on any outward capital movements whatsoever, thus undermining one of the fundamental principles of the Community.

If the Commission were now to issue a Directive implementing the principle of non-discrimination in tax treatment, it should therefore be able to count on the support of the wider political community as well as consumer movements in the member states so that the benefits of the Single Market Programme are extended to the savings of households.

Recognising the joint nature of the transaction, the Commission could act *either* under Articles 95–98, which prohibit discrimination in the tax treatment of similar domestic and imported commodities, or under Article 100. This article provides the legal basis for harmonisation measures in the field of direct taxation.[6]

Following the Bachmann judgement and Article 73D, there can no longer be any doubt that the establishment of the Single Market in this sector of the European economy is being blocked by the discriminatory taxation laws of member states.

Unless the Commission acts, then the Community will ultimately be seen to have failed to complete the Single Market in an important part of its economy—namely the market for long-term retail savings. Such a failure will not be a marginal failure but a major failure of the programme: it was precisely from the liberalisation of this sector that much of the benefit from the Single Market Programme was expected to arise.

Notes

1 P. Cecchini, 'Studies on the Economics of Integration: The Cost of Non-Europe', Brussels, 1988.
2 Commission of the European Communities, 'Research on The Cost of Non-Europe', Volume 2, Chap. 10, Tables 4.2 and 6.1, Brussels, 1988.
3 Jonathan Hoffman, 'Towards a Single European Capital Market', CSFB Economics Dept., London April 1992.
4 Commission of the European Communities, Report of the Committee of Independent Experts on Company Taxation, Brussels, 1992.
5 Article 73D of the Treaty which states that:
   1. 'The provisions of Article 73B (the article prohibiting all restrictions on the movement of capital) shall be without prejudice to the right of member states:
      (a) To apply the relevant provisions of their tax law which distinguish between tax-payers who are not in the same situation with regard to their place of residence, or with regard to the place where their capital is invested;'
   The paragraph discriminatory force of this clause is somewhat alleviated by paragraph 3 of the same article which states that 'the measures and procedures referred to in paragraph 1 shall not constitute a means of arbitrary discrimination or a disguised restriction on the free movement of capital and payments as defined in Article 73B'. However, Denmark's failure to ratify the Maastricht Treaty provides the Commission with an opportunity to have all of Article 73D removed from the Treaty.
6 Unlike Articles 95–98, which are quite specific in their prohibition of fiscal discrimination, Article 100 is very general and provides as follows:
   'The Council shall . . . issue directives for the approximation of such laws, regulations or administrative provisions of the Member States as directly affect the establishment or functioning of the Common Market'.

Facing up to the Cost of Equity:
Changing Behaviour of Japanese Companies

SPECIAL MERIT AWARD

Summary

In the late 1980s, Japanese companies raised huge amounts of money from capital markets worldwide. Thanks to ever-rising stock prices, they could issue equity at a very low cost. The cheap money was one of the secrets of the success of Japanese business to get over the shock of yen appreciation and to have grown at 5% in real terms since 1985.

The excess finance of the late 1980s, however, now seems to affect Japanese companies. The stock market is in a slump and the new issue of equity is very difficult, if not impossible. Banks are less willing to lend because of international regulations. Investors demand more dividends on stocks. Managers cannot but wonder what has gone wrong.

Japanese managers have seldom been aware of the true cost of their equity. In fact, they did not have to think about it. The slump of the stock market and the difficulty of equity finance, however, provide managers with a rare opportunity to realize that the true cost of their equity is higher than they have thought.

The essay tries to summarize how one can understand the true cost of equity, why there was a significant gap of perception between Japanese managers and investors about the cost of equity, and how the current slump of the stock market is changing the perception. The essay also refers to the possible changes of behaviour of Japanese companies, once managers understand the true cost of equity.

The excess finance of Japanese companies in the late 1980s is an interesting case for managers anywhere in the world. If managers are not aware of the true cost of equity, they may end up making the same 'mistakes' as Japanese managers did.

Kazunori Suzuki currently works as a financial adviser for Japanese corporations at the Corporate Banking Planning and Credit Division of the Fuji Bank, Ltd. in Tokyo. He received his BA of Laws from the University of Tokyo (1986) and MBA with distinction from INSEAD in France (1990). As a Research Associate at INSEAD, he published 'Survival of Japanese Personnel Management in the New Breed Age' (*Euro-Asia Centre Research Paper Series*, 1991). His research interest lies in the strength and weakness of the so-called Japanese-style management, especially in the field of finance. He now works on the synthetic application of different financial instruments to corporate finance.

11

Facing up to the Cost of Equity
Changing Behaviour of Japanese Companies

KAZUNORI SUZUKI*

Introduction

In the late 1980s when the stock market continued to break the record high, few people dreamed of the current slump in the market. For managers of Japanese companies, the latter half of the 1980s was one of the best times in their history. Soaring stock markets and low interest rates helped them raise as much money as they wanted either by issuing equities or borrowing from banks. People believed that there would be no end to the prosperity of the financial market.

Now that the party is over, Japanese managers have started to wonder what the easy finance of the late eighties was all about. Are they responsible for the stock market slump? Were they wrong to take advantage of the boom in the stock market? Was the *easy money* that they obtained from the market really cheap?

To answer these questions, one should reassess the true cost of equity of a company. For a long time, managers in Japan have seldom been conscious of the cost of their equity. They have somehow believed that the equity is a source of cheap money.

The aim of this essay is to summarize why the perception of the cost of equity has been changing since the late 1980s and how the change will affect Japanese companies. The first section presents a short history of the Japanese equity market starting from the late 1980s up to now. The second section explains how one should perceive the cost of equity and why there was a gap of perceptions between investors and managers. The third section analyzes the recent change of investors'

* The author would like to thank his colleagues and Ryoko Wada of Fuji Research Institute Corp. for their helpful comments. The opinion, however, is entirely personal and should not be associated with that of the organization to which the author belongs.

attitudes towards stock investment, which will force managers to be more aware of the cost of equity, and consequently to behave differently in the future.

1. Short History of Equity Financing

1.1 Period of Easy Money (1945–1989)

The latter half of the 1980s in Japan was a period of *financial spree.* An unprecedented appreciation of the Japanese yen triggered by the Plaza Accord of G5 countries in September 1985 compelled the Bank of Japan to ease its monetary policy, in order (a) to prevent the yen from strengthening further and (b) to help export oriented Japanese companies to restructure themselves to be more domestic demand oriented. The Bank of Japan cut its official discount rate to the historical low of 2.5% in February 1987 and kept it at that level until May 1989, when the Bank finally raised the rate by 0.75%. Buoyed by the low interest rate, business in Japan picked up from its bottom in November 1986 and expanded until 1990 by 5% p.a. in real terms. Despite the economic growth, the inflation rate remained low thanks to the price decline of imported goods caused by the strong yen. This low inflation enabled the Bank of Japan to continue the slack monetary policy for more than two years.

In contrast to the price of commodities that stayed fairly constant, the price of two assets skyrocketed during the late 1980s period: stock and real estate. The mechanism of price rise of these assets can be summarized as follows.

Because of the easy monetary policy and the coincidental liberalization of financial markets, major companies found themselves furnished with plenty of instruments to raise money. The low interest rate of deposits made the stock investment more attractive to Japanese investors. The robust recovery of the Japanese economy from the *endaka-fukyo* (yen appreciation recession) drew the attention of worldwide investors to the Japanese stock markets. Both domestic and foreign investors rushed to buy shares or bonds with embedded equity, i.e., convertible bonds and bonds with warrants. Exhibit 1 shows the total amount of money raised in the form of equity related financing. Some foreign investors valued the warrants or convertibles so much that the yield of foreign-currency-denominated bonds sometimes

Exhibit 1   Equity Financing (listed companies)

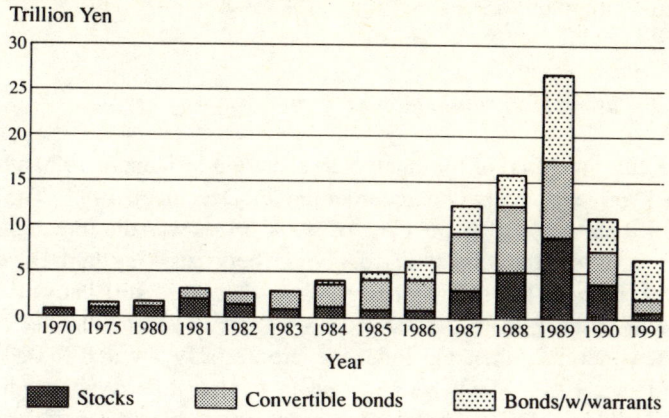

Trillion Yen

Source: Tokyo Stock Exchange

turned out to be negative after being converted into yen. Companies could raise as much money as they liked very cheaply.

Japanese banks found that major corporations were reluctant to take out bank loans because of their relatively high cost compared with equity financing. Since the slack monetary policy enabled banks to finance cheaply from the money market, banks needed to find clients to borrow from them. The new clients turned out to be smaller companies or individuals who did not have a direct access to the financial market.

The huge amount of money raised either by equity financing or bank borrowing was invested in various forms. Companies invested the money in their facilities to increase productive capacity. They also heavily invested abroad to set up branches or affiliates. The financed amount, however, was so big that these actual investment needs of companies were not enough. The money had to find its place among investment in stock and real estate markets. In those days, investors somehow came to believe that the price would never go down in these markets. Quick recovery of Japanese share prices after the Black Monday of October 1987 seemed to have confirmed the belief. Some analysts publicly said 'Japan is different! Japanese share prices will never go down!' As for the real estate, the belief seemed stronger. The Japanese were convinced that land in Japan was fundamentally scarce because of the size of the country.

Supported by these benefits, money continued to flow into the markets and pushed the prices higher, which in turn made even cheaper equity financing available to Japanese companies. The 'virtuous circle' seemed to go on forever.

1.2 Period of Hardship (1989–Present)

The current slump of the stock market started in January 1990 after the stock prices had hit the record high in December 1989. The most immediate cause of the decline of stock prices was the three consecutive rises of the official discount rate between May and December 1989. Despite the economic conditions that were still buoyant, 1990 saw the Nikkei 225 Index fall from a high of 38,915 to a low of 20,222 in ten months. Then the index hovered mostly around 25,000 level until late 1991. Many people tried to explain this dramatic drop of stock prices. The most common argument was that the stock price boom of the late eighties was a speculative bubble that was destined to burst eventually.[1]

Meanwhile, the four-year expansion of Japanese business peaked out toward the end of 1990. Company profits started to decline in FY (fiscal year) 1990 and fell further in FY 1991. The estimates of corporate earnings for FY 1992 are no less gloomy. This added to the problems of the Japanese stock market. Preceding the announcements of business results of FY 1991 in May 1992, stock prices started to drop again in March 1992. Despite the five consecutive cuts in the official discount rate, the Nikkei Index hit a six-year low of 14,309 in August, when the government announced the 'emergency economic support package'.

2. Understanding the Cost of Equity

2.1 Different Methods to Estimate the Cost of Equity

Theoretically, the cost of equity is the opportunity cost of money that is invested in equities. There are different methods to estimate the opportunity cost, which give different results. Each method reflects a different perception of the opportunity cost itself.

The first approach is to use the historical data on equity returns. The calculation is fairly easy. One can calculate the capital gain portion of equity returns by computing the geometric average of a stock index return and add the average dividend yield to get the total return of investment in stocks. The difficult part of the method is to decide the length of period over which one will calculate the geometric average return on equity. If the period is too short, the calculated returns fluctuate dramatically depending on specific events or economic trends. This could make the estimation meaningless. If the period is too long, the figure may ignore the recent changes of required returns. It is desirable that the period should coincide with that of investors' horizons of stock investment. The method is useful to understand what investors expect by investing in stocks, thus the opportunity cost of capital that investors pay. It seems a fair assumption that investors estimate how much they can expect from stock investment by looking back at the past. They somehow hope that stocks will continue to earn roughly the same return as that in the past.

Another commonly used method is to use an adjusted earnings-price ratio (E/P ratio) method (statistically the inverse of the price-earnings, P/E ratio). The method assumes that a company will maintain the current dividend payout ratio and grow by investing the rest of the tax profit in projects that will earn the same rate of return as now. To compare ratios internationally, the earnings-price ratio must be adjusted to remove effects of specific accounting practices in each country.

Another method is to use the sustainable growth rate for dividends as an estimation of the cost of equity. This method assumes the same model of dividends' growth as that of the E/P ratio, i.e., the dividends will grow in the future at a constant rate. The implementation of the method, however, is more difficult because the 'sustainability' is difficult to assess.

It is important to note that managers of Japanese companies generally have a different perception of the cost of equity. Once issued, equity is money that a company does not have to reimburse, but instead pay dividends for. The visible cost of equity is practically equal to the dividend yield.

2.2 Estimating the Cost of Equity of the Late 1980s.

An interesting question to ask is what the cost of equity was in the late 1980s when the stock market was booming.

By taking a five-year and ten-year geometric average of capital gains based on a yearly average of the TOPIX Index (*cf.* Exhibit 2), the author estimates that the return on stock investment expected by

Exhibit 2   Dividend vs Capital Gain

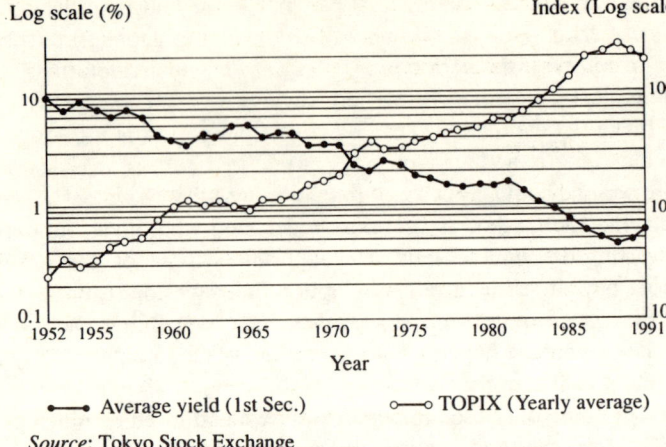

Source: Tokyo Stock Exchange

investors between 1985 and 1989 was at least around 15% in nominal terms. The result is consistent with a remark of some fund managers that they need at least 10% annual return to justify stock investment.

McCauley and Zimmer (1989) use the adjusted E/P ratio method to estimate the cost of equity in the late eighties.[2] The result shows that the average cost of equity between 1985 and 1989 was around 4% in real terms.

Porterba (1991) summarizes other studies of estimation.[3] In general, the estimation obtained by using the historical return of investment is much higher than that by other methods.

For Japanese managers, the perceived cost of equity could have been even lower. They often said during the period that issuing bonds with embedded equity would benefit them not only because the bond yield was lower, but also because they could obtain low cost money, i.e., equity, by the exercise of options. Managers seemed to regard dividends as the only price they pay for issuing equity. The dividend pay-out ratio of a share was calculated on the face-value, which in the late 1980s was normally less than one tenth of its market price. In consequence, the cost of equity for them was less than 1% in nominal terms.

2.3 To Explain the Gap of Perceptions

There was a considerable gap between what investors expected by investing in stocks and what managers thought they paid in return for issuing stocks. Such a gap seems to have persisted for quite some time, although it was remarkably bigger during the late eighties. This chapter tries to explain possible reasons for the gap, i.e., a stable corporate shareholding system and the belief of a continuous rise of share prices.

2.3.1 Corporate Shareholding

Corporate holding of stock is one of the most remarkable features that characterize the Japanese stock market.

After World War II, as companies sought equity capital, they had to find a measure to protect themselves from possible takeovers. Because the government prohibited a company from buying back its own shares, companies turned to banks, insurance companies and other companies with which they had close relationships. The proportion of shares owned by these sectors continued to increase until 1988 (Exhibit 3).

Exhibit 3 Share ownership structure

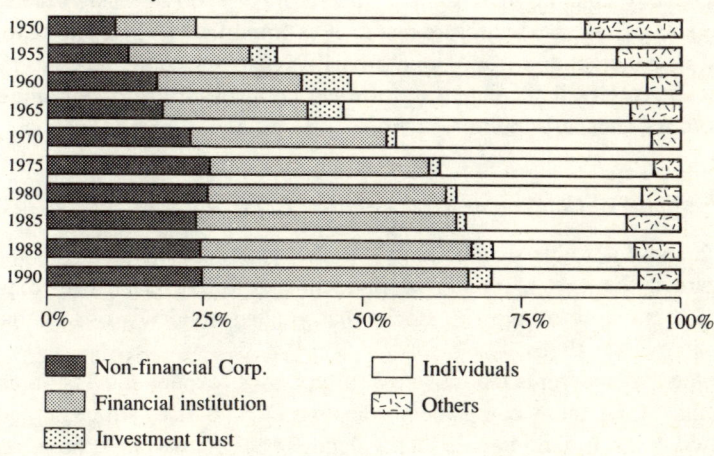

Source: Tokyo Stock Exchange

Banks and insurance companies held shares of companies to ensure a long-term relationship with them. Thanks to the regulated interest system, banks gathered deposits cheaply and lent the money to companies with the guaranteed spread. The volume of assets was almost equivalent to the volume of profits. To keep a good relationship with a company enabled a bank to monopolize the 'sure' profits that derived from transactions not only with the company itself, but also with its workers. Insurance companies had a similar incentive to hold shares because the premium rate and dividend rates were regulated.

Other non-financial companies held shares of companies closely related to them and had their shares held by them in return.[4] This cross-holding (*mochiai*) served not only to stabilize the share ownership but also to ensure the close relationship between companies. *Mochiai* is an important element of *keiretsu*, or company groups that maintain close business ties with one another.[5]

This stable shareholding structure of companies sheltered managers from takeovers. Because the majority of shareholders were financial institutions and corporations who implicitly promised not to sell shares, managers had little to worry about even if they could not meet the expected returns of investors. Stable shareholders expected more from this long-term business relationship and its consequent benefit than from the direct returns on stock investment. This is why managers regarded dividends as the only cost for issuing equity. Managers did not have to take the share price of their company too seriously because the fear of takeover hardly existed. It is important to note, however, that managers did pay additional invisible costs for equity, such as the cost of reciprocal shareholding for other companies, lost opportunities to bid for cheaper suppliers, high loan interest and insurance premia.

2.3.2 Belief of Continuous Rise of Share Prices

Although the stable shareholding structure explains why managers had regarded the cost of equity as dividends, it is not clear why other investors dared to invest in stocks that yielded dividends of less than 1% in the late 1980s.

One explanation is that business in Japan was expanding. The future profits of Japanese companies were expected to rise, which in turn would result in the increase of dividends in the future. This, however, was not enough to justify the price-earnings ratio of around 60 times during the period.

Another justification which investors preferred was a quick rise of land prices in Japan. Investors said that when the market price of land was continuously rising, stock prices must go up to reflect the increased land value of a company, because holding a stock meant that one had the right to claim assets of the company. This argument, however, should be examined with great scepticism. The logic may have applied to investors who envisaged taking over a company, splitting it up and selling some of its assets in the market. But in a country where the majority of shares were 'stabilized', an individual could hardly expect someone to takeover a company and realize the potential value of increased land price by splitting up the company.

What was more important was that many investors believed that share prices would continue to rise. As long as investors could be sure that other people would follow and pump up the share prices, and so long as the expected capital gains alone would fulfil the 15% nominal return which they needed to justify the investment, investors cared little about the increase of dividends.[6]

It seems that this *belief of continuous rise of share prices* was based on the overestimate of the growth potential of Japanese companies. In line with the belief, managers came to think that they would not have to make efforts to raise the share price of their company, which left them to worry only about paying dividends.

3. Facing Up To The True Cost

The slump of the stock market since 1990 has been changing many of the elements that enabled the cheap finance of the late eighties. This section first examines the changing behaviour of different parties of the traditional shareholding system.

3.1 Changing Behaviour of Different Parties

3.1.1 Banks

Traditionally stable shareholders of non financial companies, banks now face problems that make it increasingly difficult to maintain their shareholdings.

The first and biggest problem to date is the regulation of capital through capital adequacy ratios. Until recently, Japanese banks sought to expand their international operations without bothering too much about the profitability of loans, because they could count on the fertile domestic market where their loan spread was guaranteed.

Japanese banks, however, can no longer pursue this expansion policy because of the Basle Accord of 1988. The Accord requires banks that operate internationally to attain a risk-weighted capital-to-asset ratio (so-called 'Cooke' Ratio) of 8% or more by the end of 1992. Together with the deregulation of interest rates in the local market, the Basle Accord regulation has changed banks to be more profit-conscious. Banks now require more profit from companies either in the form of higher loan spreads or commissions for various services. They have started to analyze the cost and benefit of maintaining long-term relations with a company by holding its shares. The 'Cooke' Ratio counts the full value of company shares as a risky asset. So if banks cannot earn enough profit from the whole transactions with the company, they will be better off selling the shares that yield only 1% dividends and lending the money to other companies at the market rate of nearly 6%. Main banks have stronger incentives to maintain the relationships because they monopolize all the benefits of transactions, but lower-rank banks have fewer merits by holding shares. Such banks have started to require higher loan spreads and threaten to sell off cross-held shares if the whole transaction cannot meet their profit standard.

3.1.2 Insurance Companies

Insurance companies now face the same type of problems. The government considers liberalization of the premium rate and dividend rate of insurance companies. They are changing to be more keen on returns of their investment. The falling stock market implies that they cannot count much on capital gains, so that they now request higher dividends to be paid to justify the investment. The president of Nippon Life, the biggest life insurance company in Japan, recently requested that companies should increase their divided payout ratio.

3.1.3 Other Investors

Other investors have become more cautious about the stock investment. For the first time in more than twenty years, the Japanese stock market has seen a big slump. Investors have learned that stocks are risky assets whose prices can fall. They no longer have the illusion that stock prices will rise forever. They tend to be more selective about their investment, requiring specific profit growth or higher dividend yield.

3.1.4 Non-financial Corporations

Non-financial companies were the biggest beneficiaries of a rally of the stock market in the late 1980s. They could get over the yen appreciation and globalize their operations with the help of *easy money* that they raised by equity financing. It is true that they have a hard time finding measures to refinance the equity-linked debt whose maturity is mostly due by 1994, but the face remains that they financed themselves cheaply by selling warrants and convertibles that have turned to garbage. The above-mentioned McCauley and Zimmer (1989) estimated that the WACC (weighted average cost of capital) of Japanese companies in the late eighties was a little more than 2% in real terms.

Nevertheless, companies wonder if the easy money of the late 1980s was really good for them. A low WACC meant a low 'hurdle' for the investment. Japanese companies paid huge amounts of money to set up branches, buy foreign companies and properties. They cared little about the return on investment. A recent survey points out that the profitability of Japanese manufacturing companies has been declining since 1989 despite the growth of their sales.[7]

Now that they face a higher (and in a sense 'normal') cost of capital, they suspect that they paid too much for some investment. Recession in Europe and the US added to problems. Some Japanese companies have scaled down or even sold some foreign business of low profitability.

Slump in the stockmarket is another concern for Japanese managers. New issue of stocks has practically stopped since last year. Warrant and convertible bonds are hard to issue even at higher coupon rates than before. Banks require higher spreads on loans to ensure their profitability. Straight bonds (yield a little less than 6%) and commercial paper (interest rate around 4%) now seem to be a cheap way to raise money (*cf.* Exhibit 4). In any case, the Japanese companies will have to face up to a WACC of more than 5% in real terms.

If stable corporate shareholding starts to tumble, banks and insurance companies may become less reliable as stable shareholders, and managers may have to worry more about the threat of takeovers. There are rumours that some American companies are taking advantage of the current slump of the Japanese stock market and buying up shares of several Japanese companies.

Exhibit 4   Going back to debt breakdown of security financing
(listed companies)

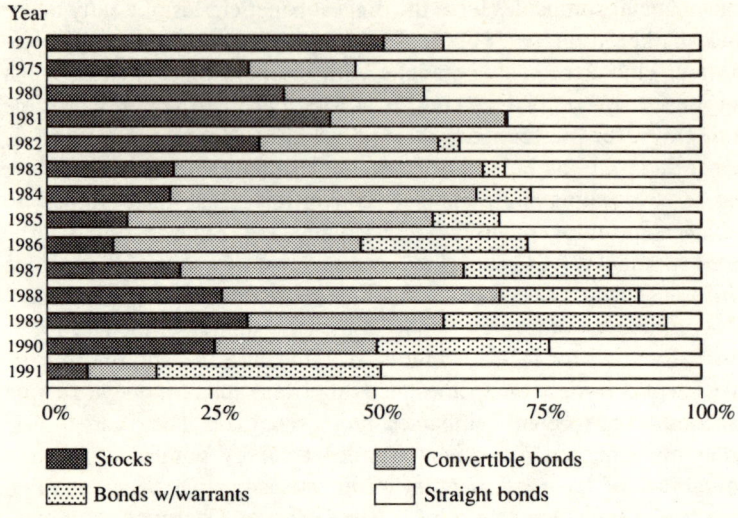

Source: Tokyo Stock Exchange

3.2 Effect of the Changing Perception of the Cost of Equity

Managers must now start to face up to the true cost of equity. Sure, equity is a source of funds that they do not have to reimburse, but it costs more than they used to think: the rising cost of maintaining stable share ownership structure, augmenting demand from investors and increasing danger of hostile takeovers: managers now see that their responsibilities to their shareholders are not only dividends but also capital gains which investors expect. They are realizing that they must augment the value of the company to raise the share price. The changing perception of the cost of equity may consequently affect the behaviour of Japanese companies.

The most important change will be that companies will be obliged to become more profit oriented to increase the share price of their company. Many theorists say that the Japanese companies behave to maximize the longer-term profit compared with American companies. They explain that a Japanese company tries to maximize their market share and kill competitors first and then 'milk' the profit in the market that they have monopolized. The explanations have some truth in them, although the actual profitability of manufacturing companies has been declining as was mentioned above. Though it is too early to judge whether the maximization of market share will lead to the future maximization of profit, it will surely take a very long time to monopolize a market, if not forever. Moreover, heavy competition from fellow Japanese companies, which tend to enter a market once one Japanese company proves it profitable, will be enough to prevent companies from milking the market. As Blinder (1991) suggested, it is doubtful whether Japanese companies really thought that they could maximize their future profit by increasing their market share.[8]

Some managers think that if they take shareholders more seriously, they may no longer be able to continue this cutthroat competition that leads to nowhere but low profitability. To satisfy shareholders who will become more demanding in the future, companies must become more profitable and pay out more dividends. Although it is unlikely that a battle of Japanese companies for a market share of lucrative business will cease, managers may set a higher hurdle rate when they choose a new project. They may start to drop existing business with low profitability. It is significant that Akio Morita, Chairman of Sony Corp., has presented an opinion that Japanese companies should stop excess competition and consider more about shareholders.[9]

Conclusion

The essay has examined how managers are becoming more aware of the true cost of equity. The process is painful. Companies pay the price for their excess finance in the past. Their stock prices are unlikely to go up by much for the time being, for there are many investors who bought shares at a high price and want to dispose of them once the price recovers. Bonds with embedded equity cost much more than before, if companies can issue them at all. Stable shareholders require more returns and otherwise threaten to sell shares.

The process is so painful that some people cannot but yearn for the recurrence of the financial fever. They turn to the government, which was responded by announcing supporting measures for the stock market in its 'emergency economic support package' of August. The Nikkei Index soared by nearly 30% after the announcement and the bearish trend seems to have stopped. Such a remedy, however, is dangerous. Easy finance is like a drug. It will ease the pain for the moment, but the cause of a disease is still there. To relieve the pain temporarily might delay the necessary operation.

What managers should do now is to admit that there is no such thing as easy money. Capital is a scarce resource which managers should use efficiently. The case of Japan should give a simple but important lesson to managers anywhere in the world. Whenever it seems that easy money is available, be sceptical and do not be fooled by its apparent cost. The true cost that you may have to pay eventually can be much higher.

Notes

1 *Asako, K., Kanoh, S., and Sano, N., 'Share Prices and Bubbles',—Chapter 3 of Nishimura, K., and Miwa, Y., (Ed.), 1990, *Share and Land Prices in Japan*, University of Tokyo Press.

2 McCauley, R. N., and Zimmer, S., 1989, 'Explaining International Differences in the Cost of Capital', *Federal Reserve Bank of New York Quarterly Review* 14.2.

3 Poterba, J. M., 1991, 'Comparing the Cost of Capital in the United States and Japan: A Survey of Methods', *Federal Reserve Bank of New York Quarterly Review* 15,3–4.

4 In general, when a bank held shares of a company, the bank also required that the company hold the bank's shares in return. The amount of shares held by the company, however, was much lower than that held by the bank, because the bank could earn profit from transactions with the company.

5 Anchordoguy, M., 1990, 'A Brief History of Japan's Keiretsu', *Harvard Business Review*, July–August 1990.

6 Investors in Japan preferred capital gains to dividends because the tax rate for capital gains was lower.

7 *Maenaka, M., 1992, Profitability of Japanese Manufacturing Companies on a Turning Point, *IBJ Flash, May 1992*, the Industrial Bank of Japan.

8 Blinder, A. S., 'Profit maximization and International Competition'— Chapter 2 of O'Brien, R. (Ed.), 1991, *Finance and the International Economy: 5*, Oxford University Press.

9 *Morita, A., 1992, Japanese-style Management in Danger, *Monthly Bungei-shunju*, February 1992.

* The original in Japanese